J.K. LASSER'S™

REFUND BUILDER
2009

D1499229

J.K. LASSER'S™

REFUND BUILDER
2009

How to Get More Money Back from Your 2008 Tax Return

Barbara Weltman

WILEY

John Wiley & Sons, Inc.

Contents

Introduction

Charles Dickens' opening sentence in *A Tale of Two Cities* described the era of the French Revolution as "It was the best of times, it was the worst of times." That description fits today's economic climate as well. It's the best of times because there is virtually unlimited opportunity for advancement in a job or to start a business, there's technology that helps you stay in touch and up to date, and you have access to information about every aspect of your financial life—the so-called American Dream (a belief that anyone can achieve his or her goals) is alive and well for many people. But now is the worst of times for so many other reasons; soaring gasoline and food prices, increasing unemployment, rising inflation, uncertain tax rules, and a growing number of home foreclosures are some of the big economic problems plaguing us today.

Today it seems that everyone is feeling a little nervous about what is going on in world markets and how they are impacted personally. When the stock market (a term that usually refers to the Dow Jones Industrial Average, or the Dow, which is comprised of just 30 stocks) goes up, many believe that the economy has turned a corner; when it goes down, that's more proof that tough times are with us. Your feelings of anxiety about the economy are not out of place, given what is happening with prices, jobs, and other key financial indicators. There is a lot of uncertainty. You're right to be concerned with what's going on and how you can weather this economic storm.

Dramatic financial changes in your life, which are indeed happening to many people today, can create stress levels that are so high as to impact your health. Stress can manifest itself in headaches, sleep disorders, difficulty concentrating, short temper, stomach upset, and feelings of anxiety and depression, and can lead to serious illnesses, including diabetes, asthma and arthritis flare-ups, irritable bowel syndrome, and clinical depression. In 1967, two psychiatrists, Thomas Holmes and Richard Rahe, developed their Stress Scale, a scoring test that measures how much certain life events contribute to stress and when stress levels put you at risk for illness. Some of the biggest stress causers are dismissal from work, changes in your financial state, divorce, and mortgage foreclosure. All of these events are happening today with increased frequency.

Serious life event changes can also wreak havoc with your financial security and personal wealth. You may be strapped to pay for ordinary living expenses, such as home heating oil or filling up your car's gas tank. Many today are living paycheck to paycheck, with no financial cushion, so that the slightest money setback can push them over the edge into economic disaster. For instance, a homeowner who experiences an illness that keeps him or her from working can easily fall behind in mortgage payments and, if this continues, could lose the home to foreclosure. Others today are facing choices about whether to purchase gas in order to get to work or buy groceries. Millions of Americans (an estimated 45.7 million) are without health coverage, so just about any medical issue can lead to onerous debt.

If there is a bright side to a dark economy, it's that good times will return. No one knows when, so the wait feels infinite. Like astronauts seeing only blackness when they're on the dark side of the moon, history shows that light (and economic prosperity) will return; economic downs don't last forever. Bad times are recessions, defined as two consecutive quarterly declines in the gross domestic product (GDP); depressions (economic downturns that last at least several years); or just short-term economic slowdowns. Are we technically experiencing a recession? It doesn't matter from the consumer's perspective, because any economic slowdown creates a personal financial impact. Regardless of how you label the current economic situation, it probably won't last long. Of the 11 recessions seen since World War II, each has been progressively shorter; the last two ran only eight months each. However, the consequences of a slowdown can last a lot longer for some, such as those who lose a job or their home; but for most people, good times are just around the corner.

Another bright side to today's tough times is that using smart strategies, including maximizing all tax breaks to which you are entitled, can get you through. You can find ways to stretch your dollar, get more income, reduce your expenses, and avoid an irreversible catastrophe, such as losing your home, by taking advantage of numerous tax rules. Simple actions can produce big and immediate results to ease your financial pain.

And yet another good thing that can come out of getting through tough economic times is learning (maybe the hard way) good financial habits. This will help you avoid problems when the next downturn occurs, as will inevitably happen. You'll have learned to create safeguards that will insulate you to some extent from future bad economies. And you'll have learned how tax rules impact just about every aspect of your life and can help alleviate some of the financial pain or discomfort that comes with losses and other adverse economic events. The information is here; it's up to you to act upon it.

How to Use This Book

The chapters in this book are organized by subject matter so you can browse through them to find the subjects that apply to you or those in which you have an interest.

Each tax benefit is denoted by an icon to help you spot the type of benefit involved:

 Exclusion

 Above-the-line deduction

 Itemized deduction (a deduction taken *after* figuring adjusted gross income)

Credit

 Other benefit (e.g., a subtraction that reduces income)

For each tax benefit you will find an explanation of what it is, starting with the maximum benefit or benefits you can claim if you meet all eligibility requirements. You'll learn the conditions or eligibility requirements for claiming or qualifying for the benefit. You'll find both planning tips to help you make the most of the benefit opportunity as well as pitfalls to help you avoid problems that can prevent your eligibility. You'll see where to claim the benefit (if reporting is required) on your tax return and what records you must retain to support your tax position.

You'll find hundreds of examples to show you how other taxpayers have successfully taken advantage of the benefit. Over the years, taxpayers have been able to write off literally thousands of items; not every one is listed here because space does not allow it. And you'll learn what *isn't* allowed even though you might otherwise think so. There are references to free IRS publications on a variety of tax topics that you can download from the IRS web site (www.irs.gov) or obtain free of charge by calling 800-829-1040. Also included are titles of other J.K. Lasser books on various topics throughout this book.

CHAPTER 1

You and Your Family

Do the old clichés still ring true? Can two still live as cheaply as one? Are things really cheaper by the dozen? For tax purposes, there are certain tax breaks for building a family.

This chapter explains family-related tax benefits, including:

- Personal exemption
- Dependency exemption
- Child tax credit
- Earned income credit
- Dependent care credit
- Adoption costs
- Foster care
- Child support
- Alimony

For more information on these topics, see IRS Publication 501, *Exemptions, Standard Deduction, and Filing Information*; IRS Publication 503, *Child and Dependent Care Expenses*; IRS Publication 504, *Divorced or Separated Individuals*; IRS Publication 596, *Earned Income Credit*; and IRS Publication 972, *Child Tax Credit*.

Personal Exemption

Each taxpayer (other than someone who is another taxpayer's dependent) automatically is entitled to a deduction just for being a taxpayer. The amount of the deduction, called the exemption amount, is a fixed dollar amount ($3,500 in 2008). However, if a taxpayer is considered to be a "high-income taxpayer," he or she loses some or all of this deduction.

Benefit ◉

You can claim a deduction for yourself, called a personal exemption. In 2008, the exemption amount is $3,500 (each year it is indexed for inflation). Table 1.1 shows you the value of your personal exemption for your tax bracket in 2008 (the amount of taxes you save by claiming it).

Conditions

There are no conditions to claiming this deduction; it's yours because you are a taxpayer and the law says you are entitled to it.

Each spouse is entitled to his or her own personal exemption. On a joint return, two personal exemptions are claimed. If you are married but file a separate return, you can claim

TABLE 1.1 Value of Your Personal Exemption in 2008

Your Top Tax Bracket	Value of Your Exemption
10%	$ 350
15%	525
25%	875
28%	980
33%	1,155
35%	1,225

both deductions (an exemption for you and an exemption for your spouse) if your spouse has no income and is not the dependent of another taxpayer.

However, you *cannot* claim the personal exemption if you can be claimed as a dependent on another taxpayer's return. For example, a child who is the parent's dependent cannot claim a personal exemption on the child's own return.

Planning Tips

If a parent waives a dependency exemption for a child, the child can then claim the exemption on his or her own return (the child is no longer treated as a dependent). This may be advisable, for example, when the parent cannot use an education credit because the parent's income is too high, but the child can use the credit to offset his tax liability (see Chapter 3).

High-income taxpayers may lose some or all of their deduction for exemptions as explained below (see Pitfalls). But the phaseout of personal and dependency exemptions is being eliminated. The reduction of this phaseout, which started in 2006, is not fully in effect until 2010.

Pitfalls

You may lose some or all of the personal exemption (as well as dependency exemptions discussed later) if you are a high-income taxpayer. The write-off for exemptions is phased out for taxpayers with adjusted gross income above a set amount; once AGI reaches a set level, no write-offs are permitted. Table 1.2 shows where the phaseout of exemptions begins and the AGI level at which no exemptions can be claimed.

Once your AGI exceeds the beginning of the phaseout range, the deduction for personal and dependency exemptions is reduced by 2 percent for each $2,500 of AGI over the beginning phaseout number. However, the phaseout is reduced by one-third. Use the Worksheet 1.1 to figure your limitation, if any, on exemptions you can claim.

TABLE 1.2 Phaseout of Personal Exemption for 2008

Your Filing Status	AGI—Beginning of Phaseout	AGI above Which Exemption Fully Phased Out*
Married filing jointly	$239,950	$362,450
Head of household	199,950	322,450
Unmarried (single)	159,950	282,450
Married filing separately	119,975	181,225

*This is prior to the one-third cut explained above.

WORKSHEET 1.1 Reduction of Exemption Amount

Use this worksheet to figure the amount to enter on Worksheet 1, line 4.

1. Multiply $3,500 by the number of exemptions you plan to claim.	1. _____
2. Enter adjusted gross income	2. _____

3. Enter:
    $159,950 if single
    $239,950 if married filing
        jointly or qualifying
        widow(er)
    $119,975 if married filing
        separately
    $199,950 if head of household
	3. _____

4. Subtract line 3 from line 2 and enter here	4. _____

5. Is line 4 more than $122,500 (more than $61,250 if married filing separately)?

☐ Yes. Multiply $2,333 by the number of exemptions you plan to claim and enter the result here and on Worksheet 1, line 4. Do not complete the rest of this worksheet.

☐ No. Divide line 4 by $2,500 ($1,250 if married filing separately). If the result is not a whole number, increase it to the next whole number.   5. _____

(Continued)

WORKSHEET 1.1 (*Continued*)

---

6. Multiply line 5 by 2% (.02).
   Enter the result as a decimal,
   but not more than 1.0   6. _____

---

7. Multiply line 1 by the decimal
   on line 6.   7. _____

---

8. Divide line 7 by 3.0.   8. _____

---

9. Subtract line 8 from line 1.
   This is the net amount of the
   exemptions you can claim   9. _____

Example

In 2008, you are single and have AGI of $285,000.
Since your AGI is over the limit of $282,450, you
cannot use any of your personal exemption. If your
AGI is $221,200, your net exemption amount is
$3,383.

You cannot claim any personal or dependency exemption
for alternative minimum tax (AMT) purposes, a shadow tax
system designed to ensure that all taxpayers pay at least
some tax. A large number of exemptions can substantially
reduce or even eliminate any regular tax. So if you have a
large number of exemptions, you may trigger or increase
AMT liability. You may wish to engage in some tax planning
to minimize or eliminate your AMT liability.

Where to Claim the Personal Exemption

You claim the exemption directly on your tax return in the "Tax and Credits" section of Form 1040 or the "Tax, Credits and Payments" section of Form 1040A; no special form or schedule is required. If you are filing Form 1040EZ, the exemption amount is built into the tax table (you can file this return only if you are single or married filing jointly with no dependents); you don't have to subtract it anywhere on the return.

If your AGI exceeds the beginning of the phaseout range, use a worksheet in the instructions for the return to figure the phaseout of your exemption.

Dependency Exemption

A fixed deduction ($3,500 in 2008) is allowed to every taxpayer who supports another person and meets other tests described below. The deduction is called a dependency exemption. However, if a taxpayer is considered to be a "high-income taxpayer," he or she loses some or all of this deduction.

Benefit ⬤

You may be entitled to a dependency exemption for each person you support if certain conditions are met. Like the personal exemption, each dependency exemption in 2008 is a deduction of $3,500.

Conditions

There are two classes of dependents: qualifying children and all other qualifying individuals. Different conditions apply to each class of dependents.

For a qualifying child, there are four conditions:

1. Being your child
2. Modified support test
3. Citizenship test (see end of "Conditions" section)
4. Joint return test (see end of "Conditions" section)

BEING YOUR CHILD

For purposes of a qualifying child, your children include your natural children, stepchildren, adopted children (including those placed for adoption), and eligible foster children (those placed with you by an authorized adoption agency or court). A qualifying child also includes grandchildren and brothers and sisters (including stepsiblings). The child must be under age 19, under age 24 and a full-time student, or permanently disabled (any age).

Your child must live in your household for more than half the year. A child kidnapped by someone other than a family member continues to be treated as a member of your household until the year in which he or she would have attained age 18.

MODIFIED SUPPORT TEST

A qualifying child must not have provided more than half of his or her own support (you do not have to show you paid more than half the child's support). Amounts received as scholarships are *not* counted as support. There is no gross income test for a qualifying child as there is for a qualifying relative explained below.

Special rule for divorced or separated parents: The exemption belongs to the noncustodial parent if these conditions are met:

- The child receives more than half of his/her support from the parents.
- A decree of divorce or separation agreement between the parents states that the noncustodial parent is entitled to claim the dependency exemption or the custodial parent signs a written declaration that he/she will not claim the exemption.

If there is no divorce decree or separation agreement with a statement on the dependency exemption for the noncustodial parent or the custodial parent fails to sign a written declaration waiving the exemption, then a so-called tiebreaker rule applies. Under this rule the exemption belongs to the parent with whom the child resided for the greater amount of time, or if equal time, then to the parent with the higher adjusted gross income. Thus, the custodial parent will usually prevail because the child is a member of the custodial parent's household for more time during the year than the child is a member of the noncustodial parent's household.

There are five tests for claiming a dependency exemption for someone who is not a qualifiying child. You must satisfy *all* of them:

1. Relationship or member of the household test
2. Gross income test
3. Support test
4. Citizenship or residency test
5. Joint return test

RELATIONSHIP OR MEMBER OF THE HOUSEHOLD TEST

The person you claim as a dependent must either be a relative (whether or not they live with you) or a member of your household. Relatives who do not have to live with you in order to qualify as your dependent include:

- Child, adopted child, or stepchild (other than a qualifying child)
- Grandchild (other than a qualifying child)
- Great-grandchild (other than a qualifying child)
- In-law (son, daughter, father, mother, brother, or sister)
- Parent or stepparent
- Sibling, stepbrother or stepsister, half-brother or half-sister
- Uncle, aunt, nephew, or niece if related by blood

Any other individual, including, for example, a cousin, must be a member of your household for the entire year (not counting temporary absences).

GROSS INCOME TEST

The person you claim as a dependent must have gross income of less than the exemption amount—$3,500 in 2008.

Gross income means income that is subject to tax. It does not include tax-free or excluded items, such as municipal bond interest, employee fringe benefits, or gifts. Social Security benefits are gross income only to the extent they are taxable (which may be 50 percent or 85 percent, depending on the recipient's income and Social Security benefits).

SUPPORT TEST

You must provide more than half of the person's support for the year (or meet the multiple support rules discussed later). Generally, this test does not present a problem; you may be the person's only means of support.

But where the person pays some of his or her own support while receiving help from you and other sources, you need to look closely at whether you pay more than half of the person's support. "Support" is different from "income." You need to look at what is *spent* on personal living needs and not what the person *receives* in the way of income. Government benefits payable to the person, including Social Security benefits, are treated as the person's own payment of support (whether or not actually spent on personal living needs).

EXAMPLES OF SUPPORT ITEMS

Clothing

Education expenses (If your child takes out a student loan that he or she is primarily obligated to repay, the loan proceeds count as the child's own payment of support.)

Entertainment

Food

Lodging (If the person shares your home, support is based on the fair rental value of the room or apartment in your home, including a reasonable allowance for heat and other utilities.)

Medical expenses (for details see Chapter 2)

Recreation, including the cost of a television, summer camp, dance lessons, and a wedding

CITIZENSHIP OR RESIDENCY TEST

The person you claim as a dependent must be a U.S. citizen or national, or a resident of the United States, Canada, or Mexico.

JOINT RETURN TEST

If you are claiming an exemption for someone who is married, the person may not file a joint return with his or her spouse. However, this joint return test is not failed if a joint return is filed merely to claim a refund and both spouses have income under the exemption limit.

Example

You are supporting your married daughter. Both she and her husband are graduate students who each earned $3,000 as teaching assistants and file a joint return to claim a refund of taxes paid on these earnings. Even though your daughter files a joint return, you can still claim her as a dependent (assuming other tests are met).

Planning Tips

As described earlier in this chapter, elimination of the phase-out of the exemptions began in 2006; by 2010, high-income taxpayers will no longer lose the benefit of personal and dependency exemptions.

MULTIPLE SUPPORT AGREEMENTS

Even if you do not provide more than half the support of another person, you may still qualify for the deduction if you contribute more than 10 percent of the person's support and, together with others, contribute more than half the person's support. Then each of the other supporters who contribute more than 10 percent must agree among themselves who claims the exemption (it cannot be prorated among the supporters).

Example

You and your two sisters support your elderly mother. You contribute 40 percent, Ann contributes 35 percent, and Betty contributes 5 percent (your mother pays 20 percent of her own support). Since you and your sisters contribute more than half of your mother's support, a multiple support agreement is warranted.

However, only you and Ann qualify since you each contribute more than 10 percent of the support. You and Ann can decide who claims the exemption—it does not matter that you paid more than Ann.

In deciding which person should claim the exemption when more than one person qualifies, the decision should be based on who would benefit more. Factors to consider include:

• Which person is in the higher tax bracket

- Whether such person is a high-income taxpayer subject to the phaseout of personal and dependency exemptions

If all things are equal, then rotate from year to year who claims the exemption (for example, one year you claim the exemption for a parent and the following year your sibling claims it).

Pitfalls

For rules on the phaseout of the dependency exemption for high-income taxpayers as well as the impact of the AMT, see earlier sections of this chapter.

If you support a domestic partner or lover and meet all of the tests, you can claim a dependency exemption only if the relationship does not violate local law. For example, in North Carolina, a man was prohibited from claiming the exemption for his live-in girlfriend because under North Carolina law this cohabitation was a misdemeanor. In contrast, a man in Missouri was permitted to claim the exemption for his live-in girlfriend because the relationship there was not in violation of state law.

If you can claim an exemption for a partner, you cannot claim one for the partner's qualifying child because you do not satisfy the relationship test.

Where to Claim the Dependency Exemption

You claim the exemption directly on your tax return in the "Tax and Credits" section of Form 1040 or the "Tax, Credits and Payments" section of Form 1040A; no special form or schedule is required. You cannot claim a dependency exemption if you file Form 1040EZ.

If your AGI exceeds the beginning of the phaseout range, use a worksheet in the instructions for the return to figure the phaseout of your exemption.

In the case of divorced or separated parents, the non-custodial parent should attach to his or her return Form 8332, Release of Claim to Exemption for Child of Divorced or Separated Parents, signed by the custodial parent.

Child Tax Credit

The U.S. Department of Agriculture estimates that it costs $178,590 for a Midwestern middle-class family to raise a child to age 17 (without adjustment for inflation). In recognition of this cost, you can claim a tax credit each year until your child reaches the age of 17. The credit is currently up to $1,000 per child. This credit is in addition to the dependency exemption for the child.

Benefit ✛

You may claim a tax credit of up to $1,000 in 2008 for each child under the age of 17. If the credit you are entitled to claim is more than your tax liability, you may be entitled to a refund under certain conditions.

Generally, the credit is refundable to the extent of 15 percent of earned income over $12,050 in 2008.

If you have three or more children for whom you are claiming the credit, you are entitled to an additional child tax credit. In reality, the additional child tax credit is merely a larger refund of the credit you are ordinarily entitled to. There are two ways to figure your refundable amount (the additional child tax credit) and you can opt for the method that results in the larger refund:

1. Fifteen percent of earned income over $12,050 in 2008
2. Excess of your Social Security taxes (plus one-half of self-employment taxes if any) over your earned income credit for the year (the earned income credit is explained in the next main section)

Conditions

To claim the credit, you must meet two conditions:

1. You must have a qualifying child.
2. Your income must be below a set amount.

QUALIFYING CHILD

You can claim the credit only for a "qualifying child." This is a child who is under age 17 at the end of the year and meets the definition of a qualifying child explained earlier in this chapter.

MAGI LIMIT

You must have modified adjusted gross income (MAGI) below a set amount. The credit you are otherwise entitled to claim is reduced or eliminated if your MAGI exceeds a set amount. MAGI for purposes of the child tax credit means AGI increased by the foreign earned income exclusion, the foreign housing exclusion or deduction, or the possession exclusion for American Samoa residents.

The credit amount is reduced by $50 for each $1,000 of MAGI or a fraction thereof over the MAGI limit for your filing

TABLE 1.3 Phaseout of Child Tax Credit over MAGI Limits in 2008

Filing Status	MAGI Limit
Married filing jointly	$110,000
Head of household	75,000
Unmarried (single)	75,000
Qualifying widow(er)	75,000
Married filing separately	55,000

status. The phaseout begins if MAGI exceeds the limits found in Table 1.3.

Example

In 2008 you are a head of household with two qualifying children. Your MAGI is $80,000. Your credit amount of $2,000 ($1,000 × 2) is reduced by $250 ($80,000 − $75,000 = $5,000 MAGI over the limit, $1,000 × $50). Your credit is $1,750 ($2,000 − $250).

REFUNDABLE CREDIT

If the credit you are entitled to claim is more than your tax liability, you can receive the excess amount as a "refund." The refund is limited to 15 percent of your taxable earned income (such as wages, salary, tips, commissions, bonuses, and net earnings from self-employment) over $8,500 in 2008. If your earned income is not over $8,500, you may still qualify for the additional credit if you have three or more children.

If you have three or more children for whom you are claiming the credit, you may qualify for a larger refund, called the additional child tax credit. You can figure your refund in the usual manner as explained earlier, or, if more favorable, you can treat your refundable amount as the excess of the Social Security taxes you paid for the year (plus one-half of self-employment taxes, if any), over your earned income credit (explained later in this chapter).

Planning Tip

If you know you will become entitled to claim the credit (e.g., you are expecting the birth of a child in 2008), you may wish to adjust your withholding so that you don't have too much income tax withheld from your paycheck. Increase your withholding allowances so that less income tax is withheld from your pay by filing a new Form W-4, Employee's Withholding Allowance Certificate, with your employer.

Pitfall

There is no downside to claiming the credit. If you are entitled to it, be sure to claim it.

Where to Claim the Credit

You figure the credit on a worksheet included in the instructions for your return. You claim the credit in the "Tax and Credits" section of Form 1040 or the "Tax, Credits and Payments" section of Form 1040A; you cannot claim the credit if you file Form 1040EZ.

If you are eligible for the additional child tax credit, you figure this on Form 8812, Additional Child Tax Credit.

Earned Income Credit

Low-income taxpayers are encouraged to work and are re-warded for doing so by means of a special tax credit, called the earned income credit. The earned income credit is the second largest program, after Medicaid, that provides assis-tance to low-income people. The amount of the credit varies with income, filing status, and the number of dependents, if any. The credit may be viewed as a "negative income tax" because it can be paid to taxpayers even if it exceeds their tax liability. On 2006 returns, 23.4 million taxpayers claimed the earned income credit, totaling $45.4 billion.

Benefit ✚

If you are a working taxpayer with low or moderate income, you may qualify for a special tax credit of up to $4,824 in 2008. The amount of the credit depends on several factors, including your adjusted gross income, earned income, and the number of qualifying children that you claim as depen-dents on your return. Table 1.4 shows the maximum credit you may claim based on the number of your qualifying chil-dren, if any.

TABLE 1.4 Maximum Earned Income Credit for 2008

Number of Qualifying Children	Maximum Earned Income Credit
No qualifying child	$ 438
One qualifying child	2,917
Two or more qualifying children	4,824

The credit is "refundable" because it can be received in excess of the tax owed. What's more, in some cases the credit can be received on an advanced basis—included in your paycheck throughout the year.

Conditions

To be eligible for the credit, you must have earned income from being an employee or a self-employed individual. The amount of the credit you are entitled to claim depends on several factors.

QUALIFYING CHILDREN

You may claim the credit even if you have no qualifying child. But you are entitled to a larger credit if you have one qualifying child and a still larger credit for two or more qualifying children.

To be a qualifying child, the child must:

- Be a qualifying child as defined earlier in the chapter under dependency exemption
- Be under age 19 or under age 24 and a full-time student or permanently and totally disabled
- Live in your U.S. household for more than half the year
- Qualify as your dependent if the child is married at the end of the year
- Be a U.S. citizen or resident (or a nonresident who is married to a U.S. citizen and elects to have all worldwide income subject to U.S. tax)

EARNED INCOME

Earned income includes wages, salary, tips, commissions, jury duty pay, union strike benefits, certain disability pensions, U.S. military basic quarters and subsistence allowances, and net earnings from self-employment (profit from your self-employment activities). Military personnel can elect to treat tax-free combat pay as earned income for purposes of the earned income credit.

Nontaxable employee compensation, such as tax-free fringe benefits or salary deferrals—for example, contributions to company 401(k) plans—is not treated as earned income.

To qualify for the maximum credit, you must have earned income at or above a set amount. Table 1.5 shows the earned income you need to obtain the top credit (depending on the number of your qualifying children, if any).

ADJUSTED GROSS INCOME

If your adjusted gross income is too high, the credit is reduced or eliminated. Table 1.6 shows the AGI phaseout range for the earned income credit. This depends not only on the number

TABLE 1.5 Earned Income Needed for Top Credit in 2008

Number of Qualifying Children	Earned Income Needed for Top Credit
No qualifying child	$ 5,720
One qualifying child	8,580
Two or more qualifying children	12,060

TABLE 1.6 AGI Phaseout Range for the Earned Income Credit in 2008

Number of Qualifying Children	Married Filing Jointly	Other Taxpayers
No qualifying child	$10,160–15,880	$ 7,160–12,880
One qualifying child	$18,740–36,995	$15,740–33,995
Two or more qualifying children	$18,740–41,646	$15,740–38,646

of qualifying children, if any, but also on your filing status, as shown in the table.

JOINT RETURN

If you are married, you usually must file a joint return with your spouse in order to claim an earned income credit. However, this requirement is waived if your spouse did not live in your household for the last six months of the year. In this case, assuming you paid the household expenses in which a qualifying child lived, you qualify as head of household and can claim the earned income credit (using "other taxpayers" limits on AGI).

Planning Tips

If you have a qualifying dependent and are eligible for the credit, don't wait until you file your tax return to receive the benefit from it. Instead, file Form W-5, Earned Income Credit Advance Payment Certificate, with your employer so that the credit is factored into your income withholding. In effect, a portion of the credit is added back to your paycheck.

Example

You are married and file a joint return. You and your spouse have one qualifying child. In 2008, if your AGI is less than $18,740, your earned income credit is *not* subject to any phaseout. If your AGI is $41,646 or higher, you cannot claim *any* earned income credit; it is completely phased out. If your AGI is between these amounts (within the phaseout range), you claim a reduced credit.

The credit is based on a set percentage of earned income. However, you don't have to compute the credit. You merely look at an IRS Earned Income Credit Table for this purpose, which accompanies the instructions for your return.

You can have the IRS figure your credit for you (you don't even have to look it up in the table). To do this, just complete your return up to the earned income credit line and put "EIC" on the dotted line next to it. If you have a qualifying child, complete and attach Schedule EIC to the return. Also attach Form 8862, Information to Claim Earned Income Credit after Disallowance, if you are required to do so as explained next.

Pitfalls

You lose eligibility for the credit if you have unearned income over $2,950 in 2008 from dividends, interest (both taxable and tax-free), net rent or royalty income, net capital gains, or net passive income that is not self-employment income.

You lose out on the opportunity to claim the credit in future years if you negligently or fraudulently claim it on your return. You are banned for two years from claiming the earned income credit if your claim was reckless or in disregard of the tax rules. You lose out for 10 years if your claim was fraudulent. If you become ineligible because of negligence or fraud, the IRS issues a deficiency notice. You may counter the IRS's charge by filing Form 8862, Information to Claim Earned Income Credit after Disallowance, to show you are eligible. If the IRS accepts your position and recertifies eligibility, you don't have to file this form again (unless you again become ineligible).

If you received the earned income credit on an advance basis and it turns out to be more than you were entitled to (for example, your unearned income for the year disqualifies you for the credit), you owe the money back as unpaid taxes.

Where to Claim the Earned Income Credit

You can claim the earned income credit on *any* income tax return (Form 1040, 1040A, or 1040EZ) as follows: in the "Payments" section of Form 1040; the "Tax, Credits, and Payments" section of Form 1040A; or the "Payments and Tax" section of Form 1040EZ.

You can check your eligibility to claim the credit on Schedule EIC, Earned Income Credit, which must be attached to your return.

Dependent Care Expenses

Many taxpayers must pay for the care of a child in order to work. According to the National Association of Child Care Resource and Referral Agencies, the annual cost of child care for an infant in 2008 ranged from $4,542 to $14,591. The tax law provides a limited tax credit for such costs, called the dependent care credit. The amount of the credit you can claim depends on your income.

Benefit ⊕ ⊗

If you hire someone to care for your children or other dependents to enable you to work or incur other dependent care expenses, you may be eligible for a tax credit of up to $2,100. More specifically, this credit is a percentage of eligible dependent care expenses (explained later). The credit percentage ranges from a low of 20 percent to a high of 35 percent. The maximum amount of expenses that can be taken into account in figuring the credit is $3,000 for one qualifying dependent and $6,000 for two or more qualifying dependents.

If your employer pays for your dependent care expenses, you may be able to exclude this benefit from income up to $5,000.

Conditions for the Tax Credit

There are a number of conditions for claiming the dependent care credit; you must satisfy all six of them to claim the credit:

1. Incur the expenses to earn income.
2. Pay expenses on behalf of a qualifying dependent.
3. Pay over half the household expenses.
4. File a joint return if you are married.
5. Have qualifying expenses in excess of employer reimbursements.
6. Report information about the child care provider.

INCUR THE EXPENSES TO EARN INCOME

The purpose of the dependent care credit is to enable you to work. This generally means that if you are married, you both must work, either full-time or part-time.

However, a spouse who is incapacitated or a full-time student need not work; he or she is treated as having earned income of $250 per month if there is one qualifying dependent or $500 per month if there are two or more qualifying dependents.

Example

You are a single mother and a full-time student with one child. You are treated as having earned income of $3,000 for the year ($250 × 12). You can use this income in figuring your credit, even though you didn't actually receive this income.

PAY EXPENSES ON BEHALF OF A QUALIFYING DEPENDENT

This is your child under the age of 13, your incapacitated child of any age, or your spouse who is incapacitated.

If your child has his or her 13th birthday during the year, you can take into account expenses incurred up to this birthday.

PAY OVER HALF THE HOUSEHOLD EXPENSES

You (and your spouse) must pay more than half of the maintenance expenses of the household.

FILE A JOINT RETURN IF MARRIED

Generally, to claim the credit you *must* file a joint return if eligible to do so. However, you can claim the credit even though you are still married if you live apart from your spouse for over half the year, you pay over half the household expenses for the full year, and your spouse is not a member of your household for the last six months of the year. In this case, you qualify to file as unmarried (single).

HAVE QUALIFYING EXPENSES IN EXCESS OF EMPLOYER REIMBURSEMENTS

Only certain types of child care expenses can be taken into account in figuring the credit. Qualifying expenses can be incurred in your home or outside the home (using a day care center). You cannot include amounts paid to you, your child who is under age 19 at the end of the year, your spouse, or any other person you can claim as a dependent.

EXAMPLES OF QUALIFYING EXPENSES

Baby-sitter

Day camp, including a specialty camp such as soccer or computers (but *not* sleep-away camp)

Day care center

Housekeeper (the portion of compensation allocated to dependent care)

Nursery school

Private school (The costs for first grade and higher do not qualify unless the child is handicapped, provided the child spends at least eight hours per day in your home.)

Transportation, if supervised (so that it is part of care), such as to a day camp or after-school program not on school premises, but not the cost of personally driving a dependent to and from a dependent care center

You do not have to find the least expensive means of providing dependent care. For example, just because your child's grandparent lives in your home doesn't mean you must rely on the grandparent for child care; you can pay an unrelated person to baby-sit in your home or take your child to day care.

The expenses you incur for dependent care must be greater than any amount you exclude as employer-provided dependent care.

REPORT INFORMATION ABOUT THE DEPENDENT CARE PROVIDER

You must list the name, address, and employer identification number (or Social Security number) of the person you pay for dependent care. No employer identification number is required if payment is made to a tax-exempt charity providing the care.

If the person has not completed Form W-4, Employee's Withholding Allowance Certificate, as your household employee, you can obtain the necessary information by asking the provider to complete Form W-10, Dependent Care Provider's Identification and Certification, or by looking at a driver's license, business letterhead, or invoice. This may seem like a lot of bother and formality for a baby-sitter, but if you want to claim the credit, you must comply with this information reporting requirement.

HOW TO FIGURE YOUR CREDIT PERCENTAGE BASED ON AGI

The amount of the credit you claim depends on your AGI. However, no matter how large your AGI, you are entitled to a minimum credit of 20 percent of eligible expenses. Table 1.7

TABLE 1.7 Dependent Care Credit Limits

AGI	Credit Percentage	One Dependent	Two or More Dependents
$15,000 or less	35%	$1,050	$2,100
$15,001–17,000	34	1,020	2,040
$17,001–19,000	33	990	1,980
$19,001–21,000	32	960	1,920
$21,001–23,000	31	930	1,860
$23,001–25,000	30	900	1,800
$25,001–27,000	29	870	1,740
$27,001–29,000	28	840	1,680
$29,001–31,000	27	810	1,620
$31,001–33,000	26	780	1,560
$33,001–35,000	25	750	1,500
$35,001–37,000	24	720	1,420
$37,001–39,000	23	690	1,380
$39,001–41,000	22	660	1,320
$41,001–43,000	21	630	1,260
$43,001 and over	20	600	1,200

shows you the maximum credit you may claim based on your AGI and number of dependents.

Example

In 2008, you have one qualifying child and adjusted gross income of $40,000. Your credit is 22 percent of your dependent care expenses up to $3,000, for a top credit of $660.

Conditions for the Exclusion

Benefits must be provided by your employer under a written plan that does not discriminate in favor of owners or highly compensated employees (for example, top executives cannot obtain greater benefits than you). The dollar limit on this benefit is $5,000 (or $2,500 if you are married and file separately).

The same limits apply to a flexible spending arrangement (FSA), which is an employer plan to which you contribute a portion of your pay to be used for dependent care expenses. This salary reduction amount is *not* currently taxable to you; it becomes tax-free income that you withdraw from the FSA to cover eligible expenses.

Planning Tip

If you have the option of making salary reduction contributions to your company's flexible spending arrangement (FSA) for dependent care expenses, decide carefully on how much to contribute each month. You can use the funds in the FSA only for dependent care expenses; you cannot, for example, use any of the funds for your medical expenses or other costs. Any funds not used up by the end of the year (or within the first two and a half months of the next year if your employer has a grace period) are forfeited; they do not carry over.

Pitfalls

If you qualify to receive an exclusion, you must reduce the amount of eligible expenses used in figuring the credit by the amount of the exclusion.

Example

You have one child and receive reimbursement from your employer's plan for the year of $2,500. In figuring your tax credit, you can use only $500 of eligible expenses ($3,000 − $2,500). In essence, once your exclusion is $3,000 for one child or $6,000 if you have two or more children, you cannot claim any tax credit.

If you participate in a dependent care FSA, distributions from the plan are treated as employer reimbursements. Like excludable benefits, distributions from FSAs reduce the amount of expenses you can use to figure the credit.

If you pay someone to care for your dependent in your home, you are the worker's employer. You are responsible for employment taxes. For more information about these employment taxes, see IRS Publication 926, *Household Employer's Tax Guide*, at www.irs.gov.

Where to Claim the Tax Credit or Exclusion

You figure the credit and the exclusion on Form 2441, Dependent Care Expenses. If you file Form 1040, the credit is then entered in the "Tax and Credit" section of your return. If you file Form 1040A, the credit is figured on Schedule 2 of the return. You may not claim the credit if you file Form 1040EZ.

If you owe employment taxes for a dependent care worker, you must file Form 1040 and complete Schedule H, Household Employment Taxes, which is attached to the return. You include employment taxes you owe in the "Other Taxes" section of your return.

Adoption Costs

Each year, about 127,000 children are adopted in the United States, with costs for some adoptions topping $60,000. Taxpayers who adopt a child may qualify for a tax credit. The amount of the credit may or may not fully offset actual costs for the adoption. If an employer pays for adoption costs, a worker may be able to exclude this fringe benefit from income.

Benefit ✚ ⊗

If you adopt a child, you may be eligible to claim a tax credit for the expenses you incur. The maximum credit is $11,650 per child in 2008. The credit is 100 percent of eligible adoption expenses up to this dollar limit.

Example

In 2008, your income is $100,000; you pay $9,000 in attorney's and adoption agency fees to adopt a child (the adoption becomes final in 2008). You can claim a tax credit of $9,000 (100 percent of your eligible costs that do not exceed $11,650).

If your employer pays or reimburses you for adoption expenses, you may exclude this benefit from your income; it is tax free to you if you meet eligibility conditions. The exclusion has the same dollar limit and income limits as the credit.

If a tax-exempt organization makes a payment to help pay adoption costs, the payment is not taxable. The payment is viewed as a gift to the recipient.

Conditions

To claim the adoption credit or exclusion, two key conditions apply.

1. You must pay qualified adoption expenses.
2. Your modified adjusted gross income cannot exceed a set amount.

QUALIFIED ADOPTION EXPENSES

Qualified expenses include any reasonable and necessary expenses related to the adoption.

EXAMPLES OF QUALIFIED ADOPTION EXPENSES

Adoption agency fees

Attorney's fees

Court costs

Travel expenses while away from home (including meals and lodging)

Nonqualifying expenses include those related to your adoption of your spouse's child, expenses related to a surrogate parenting arrangement, expenses paid using funds received from a government program, and expenses that violate the law.

MODIFIED ADJUSTED GROSS INCOME LIMIT

To be eligible for the full credit or the exclusion, your modified adjusted gross income in 2008 cannot exceed $174,730. If your MAGI is over $214,730, the credit is completely phased out.

Example

You adopt a child in 2008 and your MAGI is $194,730. You can only claim a credit of up to $5,825; half of the credit limit is phased out because of your MAGI.

Modified adjusted gross income for this purpose is AGI increased by the foreign earned income exclusion; the foreign housing exclusion or deduction; and the exclusion for income from Guam, American Samoa, Northern Mariana Islands, or Puerto Rico.

Planning Tips

The amount of the adoption credit cannot be more than your tax liability for the year. Tax liability for this purpose means your regular tax, plus your tentative alternative minimum tax (without regard to the foreign tax credit), dependent care credit, credit for the elderly or disabled, education credit, child tax credit, or mortgage interest credit if any.

However, if the credit exceeds your tax liability, you can carry the excess credit forward for up to five years.

If your employer has an adoption assistance program but you aren't entitled to some or all of the exclusion (e.g., your MAGI is too high or your expenses exceeded the dollar limit), plan to pay tax on the amount your employer pays or reimburses you. The employer is *not* required to withhold income tax on these payments. Employer-paid expenses are reported on your Form W-2.

Pitfall

The year for which you are entitled to claim the credit depends on the type of child you are adopting.

CHILD WHO IS A U.S. CITIZEN OR RESIDENT

If you adopt or are adopting a child who is a U.S. citizen or resident, use Table 1.8 to see the year for which to claim the credit for payments you make.

FOREIGN CHILD

You can take the credit only if the adoption becomes final. Use Table 1.9 to see the year in which to claim the credit.

TABLE 1.8 Year to Claim the Credit for Adoption of a U.S. Citizen or Resident Child

When You Pay Expenses	When You Claim Credit
Any year before year the adoption becomes final (or falls through)	Year after year of payment
Year adoption becomes final (or falls through)	Year adoption becomes final (or falls through)
Any year after year adoption becomes final (or falls through)	Year of payment

TABLE 1.9 Year to Claim the Credit for Adoption of a Foreign Child

When You Pay Expenses	When You Claim Credit
Any year before year adoption becomes final	Year adoption becomes final
Year adoption becomes final	Year adoption becomes final
Any year after year adoption becomes final	Year of payment

Where to Claim the Adoption Credit or Exclusion

You figure the adoption credit on Form 8839, Qualified Adoption Expenses, which is attached to your return. You can claim the credit only if you file Form 1040 or Form 1040A; you cannot claim the credit if you file Form 1040EZ.

Example

In 2007, you start the adoption process, hiring a lawyer and paying a retainer of $3,000. In 2008, the lawyer helps you work with an authorized adoption agency to which you pay a fee of $8,000 to adopt your daughter, a U.S. resident. The child is placed with you at that time. In 2009, you pay the lawyer an additional $2,000 and the adoption becomes final in this year. You may *not* claim any credit in 2007. In 2008, you may claim a credit for $3,000, the expenses paid in the prior year. In 2009, you may claim another credit of $8,650 of the $10,000 expenses paid in 2008 and 2009 ($8,000 adoption agency fee and $2,000 lawyer's fee). *Note*: If the credit limit increases above $11,650 in 2009, an additional amount may be claimed in that year.

If your employer paid or reimbursed you for qualified expenses, you must also complete this form to figure excludable benefits.

Foster Care

Taxpayers who care for children in foster care and receive funds for expenses may not be taxed on the funds. Instead, they may be able to exclude the payments they receive from income.

Benefit ⊗

If you receive foster care payments to care for a child placed with you by a state or local agency or a tax-exempt foster care placement agency, you are not taxed on the payments. They are fully excludable; there is no dollar limit.

Qualified payments include payments for the provision of foster care. They also include difficulty-of-care payments to account for the additional care required for a child with physical, mental, or emotional handicap.

However, the exclusion for foster care payments is limited to payments received for five qualifying individuals who are over age 18. The exclusion for difficulty-of-care payments is limited to payments received for 10 qualifying individuals who are over age 18. There are no limits on the number of children age 18 or under for whom the exclusion may be claimed.

Condition

Foster care payments include only those made by a state or local government or qualified foster care placement agency for the care of a qualified foster child or a difficulty-of-care payment.

Planning Tip

If you are a foster care parent dealing with a private agency, make sure the placement entitles you to exclude payments received for the care of the child.

Pitfall

Payments received from private agencies that are not tax-exempt entities, even though licensed by the state, are not excludable from income.

Where to Claim the Exclusion

Foster care payments are not reported on the return if they are excludable. If you care for more than the allowable number of children over age 18, you must include the payments in income. Report this as "other income" on your return.

Child Support

Divorced or separated parents may be ordered by a court to make support payments for a child of the marriage. Even an unwed parent may be instructed to support his or her child. The recipient of child support payments, who is typically the parent with whom the child resides, is not taxed on these payments. (The parent making the payments cannot deduct them, but paying for a child support may entitle the parent to other tax write-offs discussed throughout this chapter, such as the dependency exemption.)

Benefit ⊗

Child support payments are not taxable to the child, nor to the parent who receives them on behalf of the child. There is no dollar limit to this benefit.

Conditions

Payments for child support should be fixed. If they are set by a decree of divorce or separate maintenance or a separation agreement, they are considered to be fixed.

In addition, if payments that are made to a parent will be reduced or terminated upon a contingency related to the child, then those payments are treated as being fixed for child support. Contingencies for this purpose include:

- Reaching the age of majority (generally age 18 or 21, depending on the law in your state)
- Leaving school
- Marrying
- Entering military service
- Moving out of the custodial parent's home
- Starting to work and/or attaining a set income level

Planning Tip

If a parent is required to pay both alimony and child support but makes a single payment that is less than the total amount due, the first dollars are considered tax-free child support.

Example

Ed owes his former spouse $1,000 each month to cover alimony of $600 and child support of $400. In March 2008, Ed pays only $500. Of this amount, $400 is treated as child support; $100 is treated as alimony.

Pitfalls

The parent who makes child support payments cannot deduct them. They are not considered to be part of deductible alimony payments (explained in the next section).

If a reduction in child support payments to a parent is not specifically tied to the child's age of majority but is scheduled to occur within six months before or after such date, the reduction is treated as if it was tied to the child. This means that the amount subject to reduction is viewed as child support and not as deductible alimony. The same rule applies if you are making payments on behalf of more than one child and there are at least two reductions, each of which is within one year of a child's reaching the age of majority.

If you are due a refund of federal income tax because you overpaid it through withholding or estimated taxes, you won't receive it if you are delinquent on your child support payments. The IRS is authorized to divert your refund to the parent owed the child support payments as long as the state provides notice to you and a procedure you can follow to contest this action.

Where to Claim the Exclusion

Child support payments received need not be reported on the return.

Alimony

Taxpayers who are required by a court to make payments to a spouse or former spouse can deduct such payments. The payments may be called alimony, support, or spousal maintenance, depending on state law (called "alimony" here for convenience). The tax law in most cases imposes symmetry on the treatment of alimony so that the government effectively comes out even; the spouse receiving the payments reports them as income while the spouse making the payments gets to deduct them.

Benefit ➊

If you make payments to a spouse or former spouse for alimony, support, or spousal maintenance, you can deduct the payments if certain conditions are met. There is no dollar limit on this deduction. The deduction is claimed as an adjustment to gross income; you do not have to itemize your other deductions to write off alimony payments you make.

Conditions

There are four conditions that must be met for payments made to a spouse or former spouse to be considered alimony.

1. Amounts must be paid pursuant to a legal requirement, such as a court decree.
2. Payments must be made in cash.
3. You must live apart from your spouse or former spouse.
4. Your responsibility to make payments must terminate on the death of your spouse or former spouse.

Typically, alimony that is deductible by the payer is taxable to the recipient—the government effectively nets no additional tax revenue from the arrangement. But this symmetry is not required. If you meet all of the conditions, you can deduct your alimony payments even if your former spouse is not required to pay tax on them (for example, your former spouse lives abroad where alimony is exempt income).

PAYABLE UNDER A COURT DECREE

You can't deduct alimony if you voluntarily make payments. You must either be ordered to do so under a decree of divorce, legal separation, or support or agree to make payments under a written separation agreement.

If the marriage is annulled and you are ordered to make payments, they can be treated as alimony if the other conditions are satisfied.

CASH PAYMENTS

You can deduct only payments made in cash. But you don't necessarily have to make these payments directly *to* your spouse or former spouse. Payments made *on behalf of* your spouse or former spouse qualify for the deduction if required by the divorce decree or separation agreement. For example, if you are ordered to pay your former spouse's rent with a check directly to the landlord, you can treat the payment as alimony if the other conditions are met.

If you continue to own the home in which your former spouse resides (i.e., own it by yourself or jointly with your former spouse) and you pay the mortgage and other expenses, only some of these expenses qualify as deductible alimony— even if you are required to make the payments under the terms of a divorce decree or separation agreement. If you own the home, you benefit from the payment of the mortgage, real estate taxes, and other maintenance on the property and cannot deduct these payments. If you own the home jointly, only one-half of your payments can be treated as alimony because only one-half benefits your spouse or former spouse. (Of course, you can deduct mortgage interest and real estate taxes as itemized deductions as explained in Chapter 4.)

LIVING APART

You and your spouse or former spouse must not live in the same household. This means separate residences; merely having separate bedrooms in the same home is not good enough for payments to be treated as alimony.

However, payments made while you are preparing to leave can be deducted. There is a one-month limit so that only payments made within one month prior to your departure can be treated as alimony. If it takes you longer to move out, your earlier payments are not deductible.

PAYMENT RESPONSIBILITY ENDS ON DEATH

Your responsibility to make payments to your spouse or former spouse must end if that person dies. If your obligation to make payments continues beyond the recipient's death (for example, you must continue to pay until total payments reach a set amount), you cannot treat *any* of the payments as alimony (even those made before death).

Generally, the divorce decree should state that your obligation to make payments ends on the recipient's death. But this isn't necessary as long as this condition is part of the law in your state.

The fact that your estate continues to be liable for payments after your death does not prevent you from treating your payments as alimony.

Planning Tip

Don't voluntarily increase your payments. If you want to ensure that increased payments qualify as deductible alimony, you need to amend the court order or separation agreement to incorporate the change.

Pitfalls

Payments made to someone who was never legally your spouse cannot be treated as alimony. For example, if you make payments to a domestic partner, you cannot deduct them even though they otherwise have all the earmarks of alimony.

Property settlements are not deductible. If you make payments that are reduced in the third year by $15,000 or more, you may lose some of the deductions you've already claimed. This reduction is viewed as front-loading—trying to make a property settlement appear to be alimony so that you can deduct it (a property settlement isn't deductible).

In effect, deductible payments in year one and year two are recaptured in the third year if payments decline by more than $15,000. The recipient removes them from income and you lose your deductions, and this is reported on the return for the third year (you don't go back and amend the returns in years one and two).

Where to Claim the Deduction

The deduction for alimony payments is claimed on Form 1040 in the section labeled "Adjusted Gross Income." You cannot deduct alimony if you file Form 1040A or Form 1040EZ.

There is no separate form or schedule to complete when deducting alimony. However, you *must* include the recipient's Social Security number on your return (to allow the IRS to cross-check whether the recipient reported the alimony as income).

CHAPTER 2

Medical Expenses

The cost of health care continues to escalate faster than the rate of inflation. Insurance premiums are soaring (15 percent per year increases are not uncommon), and, in many cases, employer coverage is declining. About 47 million Americans now have no health insurance at all. The bottom line is that it's probably costing you more to pay your medical bills. What can you do? Fortunately, the tax law provides you with some relief by allowing you to treat your medical expenses in special tax-advantaged ways.

This chapter covers:

- Itemized medical expenses
- Self-employed health insurance deduction
- Health insurance credit for eligible recipients
- Long-term care coverage

- Flexible spending arrangements for health care
- Health reimbursement arrangements
- Health Savings Accounts (HSAs)
- Archer Medical Savings Accounts (MSAs)
- COBRA coverage
- Medicare
- Continuing care facilities and nursing homes
- Accelerated death benefits
- Decedent's final illness

To learn more about medical and dental expenses, see IRS Publication 502, *Medical and Dental Expenses* and IRS Publication 969, *Health Savings Accounts and Other Tax-Favored Health Plans*.

Itemized Medical Expenses

Medical care for most Americans today is very costly. Even those with insurance still pay out-of-pocket for many things, including co-payments, noncovered procedures, and, often, the insurance premiums themselves. About 47 million Americans have *no* medical coverage. The tax law recognizes that medical costs, even though they are personal expenses, should be deductible if they exceed a set percentage of your income.

Benefit

If you itemize deductions (instead of claiming the standard deduction), you can write off medical expenses that are not covered by insurance, employer payments, or government programs to the extent they exceed 7.5 percent of adjusted gross income.

Example

Your adjusted gross income is $100,000. You have $8,000 of medical costs that are not covered by insurance. You can deduct $500—the first 7.5 percent ($7,500) is nondeductible.

There is no dollar limit on what you can deduct for medical expenses (once you pass the 7.5 percent of AGI threshold).

Conditions

To be treated as qualified medical expenses, payments must be for the diagnosis, cure, mitigation, treatment, or prevention of disease or any treatment that affects a part or function of your body.

Deductible expenses include those paid not only for yourself but also for a spouse and dependents. A dependent, for this purpose, includes not only someone for whom you claim a dependency exemption but also someone you could have claimed the exemption for except for the fact that the person has gross income in excess of the exemption amount ($3,500 in 2008).

Example

In 2008, you provide more than half of your mother's support, including the payment of all her medical expenses. Her gross income is $12,000 so you cannot claim her as a dependent. You can, however, include your payment of her medical expenses with yours when figuring your medical expense deduction.

Examples of Deductible Medical Expenses
PROFESSIONAL SERVICES

Annual physical

Chiropodist

Chiropractor

Christian Science practitioner

Dermatologist

Dentist

Full body scans

Gynecologist

Neurologist

Nurse, including board, wages, and employment taxes on wages

Nurse's aide for an elderly person in need of supervision and assistance

Obstetrician

Ophthalmologist

Optician

Optometrist

Osteopath

Pediatrician

Physician

Physiotherapist

Plastic surgeon for medically necessary surgery

Podiatrist

Practical nurse

Psychiatrist

Psychoanalyst

Psychologist

Registered nurse

Surgeon

DENTAL SERVICES

Artificial teeth

Cleaning teeth

Dental X rays

Extracting teeth

Filling teeth

Gum treatment

Oral surgery

Orthodontia

EQUIPMENT AND SUPPLIES

Abdominal supports

Arches

Artificial eyes and limbs

Autoette

Back supports

Blood sugar test kit

Braces

Braille books and magazines

Contact lenses

Crutches

Elastic hosiery

Eyeglasses

Hearing aids

Heating devices

Home exercise equipment for doctor-prescribed weight loss

Home pregnancy test

Invalid chair

Iron lung

Mattress to alleviate arthritic condition

Orthotics and orthopedic shoes (but only the excess over the cost of regular shoes)

Oxygen or oxygen equipment to relieve breathing problems caused by a medical condition

Reclining chair if prescribed by a doctor

Repair of special telephone equipment for someone who is hearing impaired

Sacroiliac belt

Seeing-eye dog and its maintenance

Splints

Telephone-teletype costs and television adapter for closed-caption service for someone who is hearing impaired

Television adapter to display the audio part of programs as subtitles for the hearing impaired

Truss

Wheelchair

Whirlpool baths prescribed by a doctor

Wig advised by a doctor as essential to the mental health of a person who lost all hair from disease

HOME IMPROVEMENTS[1]

Air conditioner where necessary for relief from an allergy or for relieving difficulty in breathing

Cost of installing stair-seat elevator for a person with a heart condition

Fluoridation unit

Lead-based paint removal to prevent a child with lead poisoning from eating the paint (but not the cost of repainting the scraped area)

Ramps for wheelchair access

Swimming pool

---

[1]The amount of home improvements treated as a deductible medical expense usually is limited to the extent they do not increase the home's value. However, this limitation does not apply to improvements necessary to cope with a disability (e.g., a ramp or railing for someone who is wheelchair-bound).

INSURANCE

Blue Cross and Blue Shield

Contact lens replacement insurance

Health insurance premiums you pay to cover hospital, surgical, and other medical expenses (Health insurance paid by your employer is not deductible by you, but you aren't taxed on this benefit.)

Long-term care insurance to the extent permitted for your age (explained later in this chapter)

Medicare Part B (and Medicare Part A for those not covered by Medicare)

Medicare Part D

Medigap (supplemental Medicare insurance)

Membership in a medical service cooperative

Student health fee

MEDICINE AND DRUGS

Birth control pills

Insulin

Prescription drugs

Viagra if medically prescribed

TESTS

Blood tests

Cardiograms

Metabolism tests

Spinal fluid tests

Sputum tests

Stool examinations

Urine analyses

X-ray examinations

TREATMENTS AND PROGRAMS

Abortion

Alcoholism inpatient's treatment at a therapeutic center

Acupuncture

Blood transfusion

Breast reconstructive surgery following a mastectomy

Childbirth classes for expectant mothers

Childbirth delivery

Clarinet lessons advised by a dentist for the treatment of tooth defects

Convalescent home—for medical treatment only

Diathermy

Drug treatment center—inpatient care costs

Egg donor fees (including legal fees for preparation of a contract between the taxpayer and the donor)

Electroshock therapy

Fertility treatments, including in vitro fertilization and surgery to reverse prior sterilization

Health institute fees for exercises, rubdowns, and so on that are prescribed by a doctor as treatments necessary to alleviate a physical or mental defect or illness

Hearing services

Hospitalization

Hydrotherapy

Kidney donor's or possible donor's expenses

Laser eye surgery or keratotomy

Lifetime care (see "Continuing Care Facilities and Nursing Homes" section later in this chapter)

Long-term care costs for someone who is chronically or terminally ill

Navajo healing ceremony ("sings")

Organ transplant (including the costs of a donor or prospective donor)

Prenatal and postnatal visits

Psychotherapy

Radium therapy

Remedial reading for someone with dyslexia

Special school for a mentally or physically impaired person if the main reason for attendance is to use its resources for relieving the disability

Sterilization

Stop-smoking programs

Surgery to remove loose skin following 100-pound weight loss

Tutoring for severe learning disabilities

Vaccines

Vasectomy

Weight-loss program to treat obesity, high blood pressure, or other condition

TRAVEL

Ambulance hire

Autoette (auto device for handicapped person)

Bus fare to see doctors, obtain treatment (including attendance at AA meetings), or pick up prescriptions

Cab fare to see doctors, obtain treatment (including attendance at AA meetings), or pick up prescriptions

Car use to see doctors, obtain treatment (including attendance at AA meetings), or pick up prescriptions at 19 cents per mile for the first half of 2008 and 27 cents per mile for the second half of 2008

Conference expenses (travel costs and admission fees) for medical conferences on an illness or condition suffered by you, your spouse, or dependent

Lodging to receive outpatient care at a licensed hospital, clinic, or hospital-equivalent facility, up to $50 per night ($100 per night if you accompany a sick child)

Train fare to see doctors, obtain treatment (including attendance at AA meetings), or pick up prescriptions

Planning Tips

Payments by credit card are deductible in the year of the charge (not in the year of paying the credit card bill), so year-end charges for unreimbursed expenses (such as prescription sunglasses) are deductible in the year of the purchase.

If you don't expect your medical expenses to be sufficient to exceed the 7.5 percent floor this year, hold off on elective procedures until next year. Then you can effectively bunch expenses (this year's and next year's) into one year to exceed the 7.5 percent floor.

Pitfalls

Not every expense of a medical nature is deductible. Here is a listing of instances where no deduction was allowed by the IRS:

- Antiseptic diaper services
- Bottled water purchased to avoid the city's fluoridated water
- Burial, cremation, and funeral costs
- Child care so a parent can see a doctor
- Cosmetic surgery *unless* it is medically necessary (For example, a nose job to improve appearance is not a qualified medical expense, but one done following a car accident to repair a nose broken in the accident is a qualified expense.)
- Ear/body piercing
- Hair transplant
- Health club and gym memberships for maintaining general good health or appearance
- Illegal drugs and controlled substances (e.g., laetrile) in violation of federal law
- Marijuana, even if prescribed by a doctor in a state permitting the prescription (it is contraband under federal law)
- Marriage counseling fees

- Massages recommended by a doctor to relieve stress
- Maternity clothes
- Nicotine patches and gums
- Nutritional supplements, including vitamins, and herbal supplements
- Over-the-counter medicines
- Premiums on policies guaranteeing a specified income each week in the event of hospitalization
- Scientology fees
- Sex change operation
- Special foods or beverage substitutes (in lieu of what is normally consumed)
- Tattooing
- Teeth-whitening treatment
- Toothpaste
- Weight-loss program to improve general good health or appearance

Medical expenses are deductible for purposes of the alternative minimum tax (AMT) *only* to the extent they exceed 10 percent of AGI.

Where to Claim the Deduction for Medical Expenses

Itemized medical expenses are reported in the first part of Schedule A of Form 1040. You cannot deduct medical expenses if you file Form 1040A or Form 1040EZ.

RECORDKEEPING

Retain all canceled checks, doctors' statements, receipts, and other evidence of medical expenses you paid. If you are deducting car mileage for medical-related travel, keep a detailed record of the date and distance of each trip in a diary, logbook, or other record keeper.

Self-Employed Health Insurance Deduction

Self-employed individuals (and more-than-2-percent S corporation shareholders) cannot deduct their health insurance costs from their business income. This means that health insurance costs do not reduce net earnings from self-employment. But these individuals are permitted to deduct premiums as an adjustment to gross income even if they do not itemize other deductions.

Benefit

Self-employed individuals and shareholders owning more than 2 percent of S corporations can deduct all of their health insurance directly from gross income. Thus, the write-off can be taken even if other deductions are not itemized.

This deduction includes not only payments for normal medical care, but also long-term care insurance. There is no dollar limit on this deduction.

Conditions

To qualify for this write-off, you and your spouse may not have any employer-subsidized coverage. This condition applies on a month-by-month basis.

Example

If you (or your spouse) are eligible for employer-subsidized coverage in January but opt to pay your own coverage that month, you do not qualify for the deduction. But if, in February, you are no longer qualified under the employer plan, you can deduct your premium for this month.

Also, the deduction cannot exceed the net earnings from the business in which the medical insurance plan is established. These earnings may not be aggregated with earnings from other businesses. For S corporation shareholders, the deduction cannot be more than wages from the corporation (if this was the business in which the insurance plan was established).

Planning Tips

You can claim the deduction whether you buy the insurance through the business or individually, as long as you meet the conditions explained earlier.

If you are paying for your medical insurance, you may wish to combine this with a Health Savings Account (explained later in this chapter).

Pitfalls

The deduction does not offset business expenses. Thus, it does not reduce self-employment income subject to self-employment tax.

In the case of S corporation shareholders owning more than two percent of the corporation, the shareholder can deduct his or her premiums from gross income only if the corporation pays the premiums or reimburses the shareholder for the premiums *and* includes the premiums as wages on the shareholder's Form W-2. In the past, the IRS had required that the corporation take out the policy, but this is no longer required.

Where to Claim the Self-Employed Health Insurance Deduction

The deduction is claimed in the "Adjusted Gross Income" section on Form 1040 (whether or not you itemize other medical expenses).

You cannot claim the self-employed health insurance deduction if you file Form 1040A or Form 1040EZ.

Health Insurance Credit for Eligible Recipients

Certain individuals may be casualties of trade agreements or changing economic situations that shift jobs offshore. In recognition of this fact, Congress has created a special tax credit designed to help pay for certain types of health insurance for affected workers.

Benefit

If you qualify, the government pays 65 percent of your health insurance premiums for COBRA (Consolidated Omnibus Budget Reconciliation Act of 1986) continuation coverage or insurance through a state-run program (through a tax credit to which you are entitled); you pay the balance of the premiums from your own pocket. There is no dollar limit on the credit you can claim or any restrictions on claiming the credit because of your income level.

Example

If your annual premium is $6,000, your tax credit is $3,900 (65 percent of $6,000).

Conditions

To claim the credit, you must meet two conditions:

1. You are an eligible recipient ("eligible individual").
2. You pay for certain health care coverage ("qualifying health insurance").

ELIGIBLE INDIVIDUAL

To be an eligible individual, you must fall within either of two categories:

1. You are a worker who lost your job due to foreign trade competition. You must be treated as someone eligible to receive a trade adjustment allowance (TAA) or an alternative TAA (or who would have received a TAA but you have not exhausted your unemployment benefits).
2. You are a retiree age 55 or older receiving benefits from the Pension Benefit Guaranty Corporation (you are called a PBGC pension recipient). This means that to claim the credit for 2008, you must have been born before 1953.

You can claim the credit if your spouse or dependent is an eligible individual. If you file a joint return, only one spouse has to meet eligibility conditions. You cannot claim the credit if you can be claimed as another taxpayer's dependent.

Eligibility is determined on a month-by-month basis. You are eligible in a month if, as of the first day of the month, you meet eligibility requirements. You may, for example, only be entitled to a credit for a portion of the year (the months in which you are an eligible individual).

You do not qualify if you are imprisoned under federal, state, or local authority.

As a practical matter, you don't have to determine whether you're an eligible individual; the government does this for you. It will send you Form 8887, Health Insurance Credit Eligibility Certificate, stating that you are an eligible TAA, alternative TAA, or PBGC pension recipient.

QUALIFYING HEALTH INSURANCE

Even if you are an eligible individual, you do not qualify for the credit if you have health coverage under Medicare Part A, Medicare Part B, Medicaid, State Children's Health Insurance Program (S-CHIP), Federal Employees Health Benefit Plan (FEHBP), Tricare (for certain military personnel and their families), or any coverage if at least 50 percent is paid by your (or your spouse's) employer.

EXAMPLES OF QUALIFYING HEALTH INSURANCE

Certain state-sponsored health insurance if the state elects to have it apply.

COBRA (see later in this chapter).

Coverage under a group plan available through the employment of your spouse.

Coverage under individual health insurance, provided you were covered during the entire 30-day period that ends on the date you separated from the employment that makes you an eligible individual.

Planning Tips

You can include as part of the credit any distributions taken from an Archer Medical Savings Account or a Health Savings Account (discussed later in this chapter) to pay qualified health insurance coverage.

You can claim the credit in advance of filing your tax return and are entitled to it even if you don't owe any taxes. As long as you obtain the proper certification, you pay only 35 percent of your health insurance premiums and the federal government pays the other 65 percent. Certification is made by obtaining Form 8887, Health Insurance Credit Eligibility Certificate.

Of course, you cannot claim a tax credit on your tax return if the credit has been obtained on an advance basis by means of government payment of your health insurance. The amount of the credit you claim on your return is reduced by the amount of the credit you receive in advance.

Pitfalls

Even if you are an eligible individual, not all health insurance qualifies for the credit. Examples of nonqualifying health insurance (in addition to those listed earlier) include:

Accident and/or disability insurance

Automobile medical insurance

Coverage for on-site medical clinics

Coverage only for a specified disease or illness

Coverage under a flexible spending arrangement (FSA)

Credit-only insurance

Hospital indemnity or other fixed indemnity coverage

Liability insurance or a supplement to liability insurance

Medicare supplemental insurance ("Medigap")

Tricare supplemental insurance (for military personnel and their families)

Workers' compensation or similar insurance

Check for enrollment requirements. State programs can require eligible individuals to enroll within a reasonable period after becoming qualified and deny enrollment for failure to make timely payments (and can restrict eligibility to state residents).

If you claim the credit, you cannot include the same premiums in determining your itemized medical deduction on Schedule A, your self-employed health insurance deduction, or tax-free distributions from any medical or health savings account.

Where to Claim the Credit

There are two ways to obtain the credit: by registering in advance so that a portion of the credit is applied toward your premiums (register by calling toll free 866-628-4282) or by claiming it on your return.

You figure the credit on Form 8885, Health Insurance Credit for Eligible Recipients. You claim the credit as "Other Credits" on Form 1040.

You cannot claim the credit on Form 1040A or Form 1040EZ.

Long-Term Care Coverage

Individuals who are suffering from chronic conditions such as Alzheimer's disease or are merely elderly and incapable of self-care (such as feeding and bathing themselves) require long-term care, either in their own homes or in nursing homes. According to a Metlife survey in 2007, the average annual cost of a nursing home stay in a private room is now about $77,000 (over $69,000 for a semiprivate room); it is about $186,000 in Alaska. This cost generally is *not* covered by Medicare or supplemental Medicare insurance. Only special insurance, called long-term care insurance, pays for this type of care. The tax law allows a portion of this special medical insurance to be deductible.

Benefit

You can deduct a portion of long-term care insurance premiums as a qualified medical expense (based on your age).

Benefits received under a long-term care policy generally are treated as tax-free income (the benefits are an exclusion from income).

Conditions

Since there are two benefits—a deduction for the payment of long-term care insurance premiums and an exclusion from income for benefits received under the policy—different conditions apply for each.

TABLE 2.1 Deductible Long-Term Care Premiums for 2008

Age by Year-End	Deduction Limit
Age 40 or younger	$ 310
Age 41–50	580
Age 51–60	1,150
Age 61–70	3,080
Age 71 or older	3,850

CONDITIONS FOR THE DEDUCTION

You can deduct only a portion of premiums based on your age. For 2008, the deduction is limited to the amounts shown in Table 2.1.

The premium limit is a per-person basis.

Example

Both you and your spouse carry long-term care insurance. You are age 55 and your spouse is age 52. Your annual premium is $2,200 and your spouse's premium is $1,800. You can treat $2,300 ($1,150 for you and $1,150 for your spouse) of your total $4,000 premiums as a deductible medical expense.

CONDITIONS FOR THE EXCLUSION

The exclusion applies only to qualified long-term care services provided to a person who is chronically ill and that are necessary for medical or personal care and are provided under a plan of care prescribed by a licensed health care practitioner. You are chronically ill if a licensed health care practitioner certifies that within the past 12 months you meet *either* of these conditions:

- You are unable for at least 90 days to perform at least two activities of daily living without substantial assistance, due to loss of functional capacity. Activities of daily living include eating, toileting, transferring, bathing, dressing, and continence.
- You require substantial supervision for your safety due to severe cognitive impairment.

If the policy pays your long-term care expenses, you can exclude these payments.

Benefits paid under an indemnity-type contract are fully excludable to the extent they cover long-term care expenses. If you receive benefits under a per diem contract, there is a per-day dollar limit on what you can exclude. For 2008, the exclusion is $270 per day.

Planning Tips

Since the average annual cost of a nursing home now exceeds $75,000 ($66,000 for a semi-private room), you might want to carry long-term care coverage to pay some or all of this cost if it arises. The younger you are when you purchase the policy, the smaller your annual premiums will be (they are fixed at the time of purchase and generally do not increase thereafter).

Long-term care insurance may be available as an employee fringe benefit under your company's cafeteria plan. If you opt for this coverage, you are not taxed on this benefit.

If you add a long-term care rider to a life insurance or annuity contract, the portion of the premium related to long-term care may qualify as a deductible medical expense (within the limits discussed in this section).

States may provide their own benefit for long-term care insurance. In New York, for example, there is a 20 percent tax credit, with no age or dollar limitations.

Pitfall

Since long-term care insurance usually pays a fixed dollar amount and, hopefully, you won't need long-term care for many years to come, it can be difficult to know how much insurance to carry. Consider including a cost-of-living rider to adjust your dollar coverage for inflation.

Where to Claim the Deduction and/or Exclusion

The deduction for long-term care insurance premiums is treated like other deductible medical expenses. Generally, they are included with your other itemized medical expenses (up to your allowable dollar limit). However, if you are self-employed, you can include this amount with your other medical insurance claimed as part of the self-employed health insurance deduction, which is an adjustment to gross income.

If you receive benefits under a long-term care policy that are fully excludable, you do not have to report anything on your return. But if you are limited in what you can exclude (as explained earlier), excess benefits are reported as "Other Income" on Form 1040.

Flexible Spending Arrangements for Health Care

Companies are increasingly forced to make employees pay for some or all of their medical expenses. But they can assist them by creating special arrangements, called flexible spending arrangements, that enable employees to pay for medical expenses on a pretax basis. This means employees can dedicate some of their wages to special accounts used for medical expenses. Amounts put into these accounts are not currently taxed. Contribution limits are not fixed by the tax law; they are set by the terms of the companies' plans.

Benefit ⊗

Businesses can set up flexible spending arrangements (FSAs) to allow employees to pay for expenses not covered by insurance on a pretax basis. At the start of the year employees agree to a salary reduction amount as their contribution to the FSA. These amounts are not treated as taxable compensation and are not subject to Social Security and Medicare (FICA) taxes. Employees then use these amounts anytime during the year to pay for medical costs, including health insurance premiums or other expenses not covered by insurance, such as orthodontia and prescription eyeglasses.

For purposes of health FSAs, reimbursable medical expenses include over-the-counter medications (such as antacids, pain relievers, allergy medications, and cold remedies), but not items used for general good health (such as dietary supplements).

Conditions

The plan (not the IRS) sets the limits on how much you can commit to the FSA each year. It may be fixed as a percentage of your compensation (e.g., up to 6 percent). Ask your plan administrator for details on your contribution limits and the deadline for signing up each year (just because you were in the FSA this year does not automatically cover you for next year; you may be required to complete the same paperwork all over again).

Planning Tips

You can tap into your annual contribution at any time during the year (even before you have fully paid into the FSA).

Example

In January you agree to contribute $1,800 for the year, which is $150 each month, to your company's FSA. In February, when you have contributed only $300, you pay a dental bill of $1,500 that is not covered by insurance. You submit the paid bill to your plan administrator and receive the full reimbursement of $1,500.

Decide carefully how much you wish to contribute for the year. You generally cannot change your monthly salary reduction during the year. If you fail to use up all of your contribution during the year or by the end of the plan's grace period (if any), you lose this money forever. You generally cannot carry it over to next year or withdraw the unused amount as cash. You may see this referred to as the "use it or lose it" rule (but see grace period below). Your medical expenses for the previous year may give you an idea of what your needs will be so you can set your salary reduction amount at a rate that you expect to fully utilize.

Your employer can adopt an IRS-approved grace period of up to two and a half months. If so, you have up to March 15, 2009, to incur medical expenses that can be reimbursed out of your 2008 FSA amounts.

Example

In 2008, you contribute $200 per month to your FSA. At the end of December you have used up only $2,000 of this amount. Assuming your employer adopted the IRS grace period, you have until March 15, 2009, to incur additional medical expenses of $400 so you can use up your account. If you incur $600 of medical expenses between January 1, 2009, and March 15, 2009, the first $400 is applied against your 2008 FSA contributions; the balance is applied against your 2009 FSA contributions (assuming you have agreed to these contributions).

An employer can transfer funds in an FSA to an employee's Health Savings Account (HSA). The limit on the transfer is the lesser of the account balance on the date of transfer or on September 21, 2006. This is a one-time opportunity.

Reservists called to active duty can take penalty-free withdrawals from their FSAs for any purpose (not just medical) after June 17, 2008.

Pitfalls

As just mentioned, FSAs operate on a use-it-or-lose-it basis. If you contribute more than your covered medical expenses for the year and cannot use it up in the contribution year or grace period (if applicable), you can't get the money back. Don't agree to a salary reduction amount in excess of what you reasonably expect to use for medical expenses.

FSAs cannot pay for any expenses that would not qualify as a deductible medical expense. For example, FSAs cannot be used to pay for cosmetic surgery (unless it is medically necessary—for example, to correct a birth defect).

Where to Claim the Benefit

Since this benefit is an exclusion from income, you do not have to report anything on your return. Compensation reported on your Form W-2 is reduced to the extent of your FSA contributions.

However, you are required to account to the FSA administrator in order to receive payments from the plan. For example, you may be asked to submit a paid bill for prescription sunglasses in order to receive reimbursement from the FSA, and the bill must be submitted within a certain period after incurring the expense. Talk to your plan administrator for rules on how to obtain reimbursements from the plan.

Health Reimbursement Arrangements

Companies are continually looking for ways to reduce their health care costs for employees. Within the past few years, a new type of plan, called a health reimbursement arrangement, has been created under which companies set aside a fixed dollar amount for each employee (employees do not pay anything toward these plans). An employee can use funds in his or her account within the plan to pay for medical costs without being taxed when funds are contributed or when they are withdrawn for approved medical expenses.

Benefit

Employers may set up health reimbursement arrangements (HRAs) to allow employees to pay for unreimbursed medical expenses without any cost to them. Here's how they work. The company sets up accounts for each employee and contributes a flat dollar amount. You are not taxed on employer contributions. Similarly, when you use funds in your account to cover your medical costs, you are not taxed on withdrawals. There is no dollar limit on employer contributions on your behalf, nor on amounts you can withdraw tax free to pay for medical expenses.

Condition

Your company (not the IRS) sets any and all participation requirements, so talk with the HRA administrator about anything you must do to participate in and receive reimbursements from the HRA.

Planning Tips

You can use the funds in your account whenever you need to within the year. Any amounts remaining in the account at year-end automatically carry over to the next year and can be used to cover your future medical expenses.

Funds in an HRA can be transferred by an employer to an employee's Health Savings Account (HSA). The limit on the transfer is the lesser of the account balance on the date of transfer or on September 21, 2006. This is a one-time opportunity.

Pitfall

There are no pitfalls for participating in your company's HRA. You are receiving a tax-free fringe benefit to the extent you use the coverage under the HRA.

Where to Claim the Benefit

Since this benefit is an exclusion from income, you do not have to report anything on your return.

However, you are required to account to the HRA administrator in order to receive payments from the plan. For example, you may be asked to submit a paid bill for prescription sunglasses in order to receive reimbursement from the HRA. Talk to the plan administrator for rules on how to obtain reimbursement.

Health Savings Accounts

Individuals who are covered by health insurance policies with high deductibles may be eligible to contribute money to a special savings account, called a Health Savings Account (HSA). About 47 million Americans are currently uninsured, and HSAs may be a way for them to obtain needed health coverage on an affordable basis. There are more than 6 million people who now have HSAs, and predictions put the number at 24 million by 2010.

Contributions to the account are tax deductible. Earnings on the account are not subject to immediate tax. If withdrawals are made to pay for medical expenses, they are fully tax free. Otherwise withdrawals are taxable and subject to a 10 percent penalty unless taken when age 65 or older or disabled. Spouses who inherit an account can roll over the funds tax free.

Benefit ⊗ ⬆

If you have a "high-deductible" health insurance policy (defined in "Conditions" section), you can contribute to a special savings account. Benefits to HSAs include:

- Contributions within set limits are deductible as an adjustment to gross income (you do not have to itemize deductions to claim this benefit). See Table 2.2 for 2008 limits. The limits for those under age 55 will be indexed for inflation; the additional contribution limits for those age 55 and older is $900 in 2008 and $1,000 in 2009.

- Interest or other earnings in the account are tax deferred.

- Withdrawals used to pay medical costs are tax free.

TABLE 2.2 Health Savings Account Contribution Limits for 2008

Your Age	Self-Only Plan	Family Plan
Under age 55	$2,900	$5,800
55 or older	$3,800	$6,700

Conditions

To contribute to an HSA, you must meet two conditions:

1. You are not covered by Medicare.
2. You are covered by a high-deductible health insurance policy.

MEDICARE

HSAs are designed to cover individuals who do not qualify for Medicare. Therefore, you are ineligible for an HSA once you are covered by Medicare. Since determination of eligibility is made month-by-month, you may be qualified for a deduction for the portion of the year before you are covered by Medicare.

QUALIFYING HIGH-DEDUCTIBLE HEALTH INSURANCE

You must have a high-deductible health insurance policy for at least some time in 2008. This can be a policy that you have obtained personally or coverage provided by your employer. The determination of whether you have such coverage is made on the first day of the month.

A high-deductible policy is one that falls within certain limits. (See Table 2.3.).

TABLE 2.3 2008 High-Deductible Policy Limits

	Self-Only Coverage	Family Coverage
Annual deductible at least	$1,100	$ 2,200
Limit on expenses	$5,600	$11,200

You cannot have any other health coverage, other than accident insurance, dental care, disability coverage, disease-specific coverage (such as cancer insurance), long-term care, vision care, and workers' compensation.

Like individual retirement accounts (IRAs), contributions to HSAs can be made up to the due date for the return (without extensions). For example, contributions for 2008 can be made up to April 15, 2009.

Tax-Free Withdrawals

Only account distributions used to pay qualified medical expenses are tax free. Qualified medical expenses include:

- Any expense that could be claimed as an itemized medical deduction (see the section earlier in this chapter)
- COBRA premiums
- Over-the-counter medications
- Premiums for long-term care insurance
- Periodic health evaluations, such as annual physicals
- Routine prenatal and well-child care
- Child and adult immunizations
- Tobacco cessation programs
- Obesity weight-loss programs
- Screening services, such as those listed

Examples of Screening Services Treated as Medical Expenses for HSAs

CANCER SCREENING

Breast cancer (e.g., mammogram)

Cervical cancer (e.g., Pap smear)

Colorectal cancer

Oral cancer

Ovarian cancer

Prostate cancer (e.g., prostate-specific antigen [PSA] test)

Skin cancer

Testicular cancer

Thyroid cancer

HEART AND VASCULAR DISEASES SCREENING

Abdominal aortic aneurysm

Carotid artery stenosis

Coronary heart disease

Hemoglobinopathies

Hypertension

Lip disorders

INFECTIOUS DISEASES SCREENING

Bacteriuria

Chlamydial infection

Gonorrhea

Hepatitis B virus infection

Hepatitis C

Human immunodeficiency virus (HIV) infection

Syphilis

Tuberculosis infection

MENTAL HEALTH CONDITIONS AND SUBSTANCE ABUSE SCREENING

Dementia

Depression

Drug abuse

Family violence

Problem drinking

Suicide risk

METABOLIC, NUTRITIONAL, AND ENDOCRINE CONDITIONS SCREENING

Anemia, iron deficiency

Dental and periodontal disease

Diabetes mellitus

Obesity in adults

Thyroid disease

MUSCULOSKELETAL DISORDERS SCREENING

Osteoporosis

OBSTETRIC AND GYNECOLOGIC CONDITIONS SCREENING

Bacterial vaginosis in pregnancy

Gestational diabetes mellitus

Home uterine activity monitoring

Neural tube defects

Preeclampsia

Rh incompatibility

Rubella

Ultrasonography in pregnancy

PEDIATRIC CONDITIONS SCREENING

Child developmental delay

Congenital hypothyroidism

Lead levels in childhood and pregnancy

Phenylketonuria

Scoliosis, adolescent idiopathic

VISION AND HEARING DISORDERS SCREENING

Glaucoma

Hearing impairment in older adults

Newborn hearing

Planning Tips

It is up to you to keep track of medical costs so that you can prove withdrawals from your HSA were used to pay qualified expenses. The financial institution with which you have your account won't ask you for any substantiation on your part. Neither will your employer if the account is set up through your company.

HSAs can be funded by a one-time transfer by an employer from a flexible spending arrangement (FSA) or by a health reimbursement arrangement (HRA), to an employee's HSA or an IRA rollover. Transfers from FSAs and HRAs are limited (as explained earlier in this chapter). Rollovers from IRAs are not currently taxed.

HSAs can be funded by means of a direct deposit of a tax refund. For example, if you expect a refund for 2008 and plan to contribute to an HSA, file your return early enough so that the IRS has time to process it and transfer your refund directly in the HSA (you must provide account information to make the transfer possible). Alternatively, use a 2008 refund to make a contribution to an HSA if eligible to do so for that year (designate whether the refund is being used to fund a 2008 or 2009 contribution where possible).

Funds in the HSA can be used for retirement savings. Since there is no tax on earnings that the account is building up, the healthier you stay (and the less you need to use account funds for medical bills), the more you'll have in retirement to use for any purpose. While the withdrawals will be taxed, there is no penalty on withdrawals for nonmedical purposes once you reach age 65.

Pitfalls

If you take withdrawals to pay nonmedical expenses, the distribution is taxed as ordinary income, regardless of your age. In addition, if you are under age 65, you are also subject to a 10 percent penalty (unless you are disabled). There is no 10 percent penalty on distributions because of the account owner's death.

If you have a separate prescription drugs benefit plan that has no deductible (only co-payments for each prescription), you cannot be an eligible individual for HSA purposes.

If you inherit an HSA and are not a surviving spouse of the account owner, you must take a complete distribution of the account and include all of the funds in your income. Check to see if you qualify for a deduction for federal estate tax on the HSA.

Where to Claim the Benefits

The deduction is figured on Form 8889, Health Savings Accounts (HSAs). The deduction is then claimed as an above-the-line deduction in the "Adjusted Gross Income" section of Form 1040. You cannot claim the deduction if you file Form 1040A or 1040EZ.

If your employer contributes to an HSA on your behalf, this is a tax-free fringe benefit; no reporting is required.

Archer Medical Savings Accounts

Self-employed individuals and small employers can set up Archer Medical Savings Accounts (MSAs) to save money for their health insurance costs by combining a "high-deductible" medical insurance policy with this special savings plan. If they have a policy that falls within parameters set by the tax law, then they (or their employees) can contribute a fixed amount to an IRA-like account. Contributions are deductible, earnings are not currently subject to tax, and withdrawals for medical purposes are tax free (i.e., contributions and earnings on contributions used to pay medical costs are never taxed). Archer MSAs are an alternative to HSAs for eligible taxpayers. The opportunity to set up new MSAs expired at the end of 2007, so contributions can only be made to MSAs set up before 2008.

Benefit

If you are self-employed or an employee of a small employer with a "high-deductible" health insurance policy (defined in "Conditions" section), you can contribute to a special savings account that can be tapped to cover unreimbursed medical

TABLE 2.4 2008 Limits on Deductibles and Out-of-Pocket Expenses

Type of Coverage	Minimum Annual Deductible	Maximum Annual Deductible	Maximum Annual Out-of-Pocket Expenses
Individual (self-only policy)	$1,950	$2,900	$3,850
Family	$3,850	$5,800	$7,050

expenses. There are several benefits to Archer Medical Savings Accounts (MSAs):

- Contributions within set limits are deductible (or tax free if made by your employer).
- Interest or other earnings in the account are tax deferred.
- Withdrawals used to cover medical expenses are tax free.

Conditions

You must be self-employed or an employee of a "small employer" covered by a "high-deductible" health insurance policy. A small employer is an employer who had on average 50 or fewer employees during either of the two preceding calendar years. If the business is new, then the employer is treated as a small employer if it reasonably expects to employ 50 or fewer workers. If a business made contributions to an Archer MSA this year, it can continue to be treated as a small employer as long as it had no more than 200 employees each year after 1996.

A high-deductible policy is one that falls within certain limits on deductibles and out-of-pocket expenses required to be paid (other than premiums) before the policy kicks in. (See Table 2.4.)

Example

In 2008, you are self-employed and have a self-only health insurance policy with an annual deductible of $2,000 and a limit on out-of-pocket expenses of $3,000. Assuming you meet other conditions, you have a high-deductible plan and can fund an Archer MSA in 2008.

You (or your spouse) cannot have any other health plan that is not a high-deductible plan. But coverage under certain other health plans will not prevent you from being able to fund an Archer MSA. Other coverage you may have *in addition* to a high-deductible plan includes insurance covering accidents, disability, dental care, vision care, long-term care, benefits related to worker's compensation, a specific illness or disease, or a fixed amount per day or other period of hospitalization.

Assuming you meet the conditions for claiming a deduction, the amount is limited to 65 percent of your annual deductible for self-only coverage or 75 percent of your annual deductible for family coverage.

Example

In 2008, you are self-employed and have a health
insurance policy for family coverage with a $4,000
annual deductible. In 2008, you can contribute
$3,000 to an Archer MSA ($4,000 × 75%).

If you have coverage for only part of the year, you must
prorate the deduction.

Example

Same facts as in the preceding example but you start
coverage on July 1, 2008, and maintain it for the
balance of the year. You can contribute $1,500 to an
Archer MSA ($4,000 × 75% ÷ 12 months × 6
months).

Contributions for 2008 must be made no later than December 31, 2008. Even though the account resembles an HSA, you do not have until tax time to fund the account.

Planning Tips

You can roll over funds in an Archer MSA tax free to a Health Savings Account. This may be advisable because of the extensive availability of financial institutions offering HSAs compared with limited Archer MSA options.

You can use an Archer MSA to provide retirement income. Money can be withdrawn for any purpose penalty-free after attaining age 65.

Pitfalls

If you are self-employed, you cannot contribute more than your net earnings from self-employment. Thus, if you have a loss year, you cannot fund an Archer MSA.

Example

You are 65 years old and, because you have stayed healthy, the funds in your account have accumulated to $10,000. You can withdraw this money to take a vacation. While you'll owe income tax on the withdrawal (because you are not using the funds for medical reasons), you are not subject to the 15 percent penalty (explained next).

If you withdraw funds from an Archer MSA for other than medical expenses before attaining age 65, the funds are subject to a 15 percent penalty unless you are disabled (or die).

WHEN YOU DIE

If you have an Archer MSA, you can name your spouse as the beneficiary of the account. Your spouse becomes the owner of the account when you die. If you designate any other person as your beneficiary, the account ceases to be an Archer MSA on your death and the funds remaining in the account are taxable to the beneficiary as income. If there is no designated beneficiary, the balance of your account is included as income on your final tax return.

Where to Claim the Benefits

The deduction is figured on Form 8853, Archer MSAs and Long-Term Care Insurance Contracts. The deduction is then claimed as an above-the-line deduction in the "Adjusted Gross Income" section of Form 1040. You cannot claim a deduction if you file Form 1040A or 1040EZ.

If your employer contributes to an Archer Medical Savings Account on your behalf, this is a tax-free fringe benefit; no reporting is required.

REPORTING INCOME

Withdrawals are reported to you (and the IRS) on Form 1099-SA, Distributions from an HSA, Archer MSA, or Medicare Advantage MSA. Funds withdrawn for anything other than medical expenses are taxable as ordinary income. Report the income on Form 1040 as other income.

If you owe a 15 percent penalty on withdrawals for non-medical purposes before age 65, you report the penalty in the section for "Other Taxes" on Form 1040.

COBRA Coverage

The Consolidated Omnibus Budget Reconciliation Act of 1986, or COBRA for short, imposed a new requirement on certain employers who maintain health insurance coverage for workers: allow workers who leave the job to continue their company coverage for a period of time (at the workers' expense). The opportunity to continue under the company's health plan means that terminated workers and other eligible people pay for medical insurance at group rates.

Benefit

Under federal law, if you work for a company that regularly employs 20 or more workers and has group health insurance, you are entitled to continue under the employer's group plan even if you leave employment (voluntarily or are laid off for any reason other than gross misconduct) or your hours are reduced below the level entitling you to employer-paid coverage. This is referred to as COBRA continuation coverage or simply COBRA. Your state may have its own "mini-COBRA" law, which may expand your rights (contact your state insurance department for details). For example, Massachusetts mini-COBRA requires employers with 2 to 19 employees to offer continuation coverage. And there is a special second COBRA election period for certain qualifying individuals.

Being eligible for and electing COBRA coverage gives you two key benefits:

1. Health insurance at an affordable group rate.
2. A deduction for premium payments if you itemize your medical expenses.

You can continue COBRA coverage for up to 18 months or until you become eligible under a new employer's plan, you qualify for Medicare, or you fail to make your COBRA payments (usually there's a 30-day grace period). The coverage period can be extended to 29 months if you become disabled within the first 60 days of COBRA coverage. Your family can retain COBRA coverage for up to 36 months if their eligibility results from your death.

You must pay the cost of the coverage, plus up to 2 percent as an administrative fee (102 percent of the premiums). But you enjoy the group term rates, which may be less than what you could purchase on your own. Your payment of premiums under COBRA is a deductible medical expense (explained earlier).

If you are a displaced worker, you may be able to claim a tax credit for your COBRA premiums, as explained earlier in this chapter.

Conditions

If your employer is subject to COBRA, you must notify the employer about a qualifying event and opt for coverage within 60 days of that event (no extensions are granted). A qualifying event includes:

- You terminate employment (voluntarily or involuntarily, as long as you are not terminated for fraud or other gross misconduct).

- Your parent has health insurance through his or her employer and you attain the age at which you no longer qualify (generally age 21 or upon graduation from college).

- Your spouse has health coverage through his or her employer and you divorce your spouse.

SECOND COBRA ELECTION PERIOD

To qualify, you must be receiving trade adjustment allowance (TAA) benefits (or would be but for the requirement that you first exhaust unemployment benefits), you lost health

coverage because of termination of employment that resulted
in TAA eligibility, and you did not elect COBRA during the
regular COBRA election period.

Planning Tip

Before opting for COBRA, see if there are less costly health
insurance options. For example, if your spouse is working,
his/her employer may offer less expensive health coverage.
Or you may be able to buy coverage through a professional
or trade association that is less expensive than COBRA.

Pitfalls

COBRA may not be less costly than coverage you could obtain
on an individual basis. You can reduce your current level
of coverage under COBRA, but you can't increase it. For
example, if you had dental coverage but now wish to eliminate
it (and the expense) under COBRA, you can do so. But if you
didn't have dental coverage, you can't add it under COBRA.

COBRA does not apply to long-term care insurance. You
may be able to pick up the long-term care policy individually when you leave employment, but your employer is not
required to offer you this coverage through COBRA.

Where to Claim the Deduction for COBRA Payments

COBRA payments are treated as a deductible medical expense (see earlier in this chapter).

Medicare

In 1965, Congress introduced a federally sponsored health
insurance program as part of the Social Security Act. This

program, called Medicare, is designed primarily to provide those age 65 and older with affordable comprehensive health coverage. Today, the program has grown to afford seniors various types of coverage options, from fee-based services to managed care programs. More than 40 million Americans are now covered by Medicare. At the time this book went to press Congress was working out details on expanding Medicare to offer prescription drug options.

Benefit

If you are age 65 or older, are under age 65 and disabled for at least two years, or have end-stage renal disease, you are entitled to participate in the federal government's health insurance program called Medicare. Your monthly premiums (whether paid directly by you or withheld from your Social Security benefits check), as well as your co-payments and deductibles under Medicare, are qualified medical expenses that are deductible as miscellaneous itemized deductions to the extent your total exceeds 7.5 percent of adjusted gross income (see the general rules on deducting medical expenses, including medical insurance, discussed earlier in this chapter). You are not taxed on the benefits you receive through Medicare.

Part A, which covers hospitalization, is free (those who did not work sufficient quarters can pay for this coverage). Part B, which covers doctors' charges and certain other expenses, requires you to pay a monthly premium. The premium is subtracted from your Social Security benefits if you are collecting benefits. Both Part A and Part B have certain co-payments or deductibles for your covered medical expenses.

There is a Medicare prescription drug plan called Part D. Certain low-income beneficiaries qualify for additional assistance to pay for prescription drugs called the Extra Help program. To be eligible, beneficiaries must have an income in 2008 below $15,315 if single or $20,535 if married and not be eligible for any other prescription drug coverage (including outpatient prescription drug coverage through Medicare managed care plans) Beneficiaries cannot have savings and resources exceeding $11,990 if single or $23,970 if married or living together. Details on the Medicare drug program can be found at www.medicare.gov.

Conditions

To be eligible for free coverage under Part A, you (or your spouse) must have at least 40 quarters of Medicare-covered employment. If you don't have the necessary quarters, you can pay for this coverage.

Part B is available to just about anyone age 65 or older (there are no minimum work requirements).

Part D is available to all Medicare beneficiaries.

Planning Tips

Medicare coverage generally isn't automatic; you must apply for it if you haven't yet applied for Social Security benefits. You should contact your local Social Security office to apply for Medicare three months before the date you reach your full retirement age so that coverage can start on time.

If you have been collecting Social Security benefits before your full retirement age (e.g., starting at age 62), you do not have to apply when you near full retirement age; enrollment in Medicare Part A (hospitalization insurance) in this case is automatic and free; however, you must then decide whether to also elect Medicare Part B (health insurance).

If you opt for traditional fee-for-service Medicare (rather than some managed care program within Medicare), you may want to purchase supplemental Medicare insurance ("Medigap" coverage). Medigap premiums are deductible as a qualified medical expense (explained earlier in this chapter).

Pitfalls

If you claim the standard deduction (including the additional amount for being age 65 or older), you cannot deduct your Medicare Part B payments since you do not itemize deductions.

If you wait too long to apply for Medicare Part B, your monthly premium will be increased. To obtain the lowest possible premium, you *must* apply either within a seven-month window extending from three months before to four months after your 65th birthday, or, if still employed and covered at work, within eight months after that ends.

If you did not sign up for Medicare Part D but were eligible to do so, and you do not have other "creditable coverage" (e.g., employer or other coverage that is at least as good as Medicare), you are penalized 1 percent per month for each month you delay. For example, if you wait 15 months to sign up beyond the deadline, you pay 15 percent of the premium as a penalty when you enroll. If the premium is normally $40 per month, you'd paid $46 per month ($40 plus 15 percent penalty). The penalty percentage continues for the rest of your life.

Where to Claim the Deduction

You deduct premiums as well as your co-payments and deductibles as itemized medical expenses (see earlier in this chapter). You must complete Schedule A and attach it to Form 1040.

Continuing Care Facilities and Nursing Homes

Elderly and infirmed individuals may require round-the-clock care because of their age or condition. Comprehensive programs in special living arrangements are now used to care for these individuals. A portion of the cost may qualify as a deductible medical expense.

Benefit

Advanced age and/or chronic illness may require ongoing daily treatment. Payments for nursing homes, convalescent homes, and sanitariums may be treated as deductible medical expenses. The deduction generally is not limited to the portion covering medical care; it also includes lodging and meals if confinement is primarily for the purpose of medical treatment.

If the main reason for admission is not medical care, you can still treat the portion of monthly fees allocable to medical care as a deductible medical expense. Typically, this applies to fees to continuing care facilities—the portion of the fees for medical care is deductible but the portion covering lodging and meals is not.

Conditions

Admission to the facility must be *primarily* for medical treatment to deduct all charges and fees. You can prove this by showing that:

- Entry was on or at the direction of a doctor.
- Attendance or treatment at the facility has a direct therapeutic effect on the condition suffered by the patient.
- Attendance at the facility is for the treatment of a specific ailment and not merely for general good health.

Planning Tip

Generally, prepayments for future care are not currently deductible medical expenses. However, you can claim a current deduction if you can show there is a current obligation to pay and you can establish the portion of the prepayment allocated to medical care.

Example

You and your spouse enter a retirement home that requires the payment of an entrance fee of $50,000, plus monthly payments of $1,000, to cover your accommodations, meals, and medical care for life. The home estimates for you that 10 percent of the entrance fee and 15 percent of the monthly fee are used for medical care. If you leave the home, you are entitled to a refund of a portion of the founder's fee. On these facts, you can treat 10 percent of the entrance fee and 15 percent of the monthly fee paid in the year as deductible medical expenses.

Pitfall

If you claim the standard deduction (including the additional amount for being age 65 or older), you cannot deduct your payments for continuing care facilities or nursing homes since you do not itemize deductions. As a practical matter, however, if you are a resident in such a facility for a full year, the cost will generally result in a large enough medical deduction to warrant itemizing your deductions in lieu of claiming the standard deduction, even with the additional amount for age.

Where to Claim the Benefit

See itemized medical expenses earlier in this chapter.

Accelerated Death Benefits

Whoever thought that life insurance could be beneficial to the person insured? Today, policies intended to provide death benefits to heirs may be used for lifetime assistance to the insured under special circumstances. Congress has acted in the wake of AIDS to allow proceeds from life insurance policies that are tapped during the insured's life to receive the same tax-free treatment as death proceeds in certain circumstances.

Benefit

If you own a life insurance policy with cash value and become terminally or chronically ill, you may be able to tap into that cash value on a tax-free basis to pay medical and other personal expenses.

There are two ways in which to use a life insurance policy to provide you with current cash on a tax-free basis:

1. Tap into the policy's cash surrender value under an accelerated death benefit clause if the policy contains such an option.
2. Sell the policy to a viatical settlement company (a company in the business of buying policies under these conditions).

Conditions

You must be terminally or chronically ill to qualify for the exclusion. You are considered to be terminally ill if a physician certifies that you suffer from an illness or physical condition that is reasonably expected to result in death within 24 months of the date of certification.

You are considered to be chronically ill if a licensed health care practitioner certifies that within the past 12 months you meet *either* of these conditions:

- You are unable for at least 90 days to perform at least two activities of daily living without substantial assistance, due to loss of functional capacity. Activities of daily living include eating, toileting, transferring, bathing, dressing, and continence.
- You require substantial supervision for your safety due to severe cognitive impairment.

LIMITS FOR THE CHRONICALLY ILL

While *all* payments received by someone who is terminally ill are fully excludable (whether or not such amounts are used for medical care), limits apply to those who are chronically but not terminally ill. The same limits for benefits received under a long-term care policy apply for this purpose. Thus, if accelerated death benefits are not more than the daily dollar limit ($270 in 2008) and do not exceed actual long-term care costs, they are fully excludable. But any excess amounts are taxable.

Planning Tip

To the extent you use accelerated death benefits for medical expenses, you reap a double tax benefit: The funds are tax-free income to you, and you can treat the payments you make as deductible medical expenses if you itemize your deductions.

Pitfall

To the extent you use your life insurance policy while you are alive, there is that much less for your beneficiaries after your death. If you have other options to cover your expenses, you might weigh your current needs against your beneficiaries' needs after your death in deciding whether to use accelerated death benefits.

Where to Claim the Benefit

If benefits are fully excludable, they need not be reported. However, if a chronically ill person receives benefits in excess of the limit ($270 per day in 2008), such amounts are reported as other income on Form 1040.

Decedent's Final Illness

There are no special deductions for someone who dies. But the tax law provides opportunities on the timing of deductions for the deceased. Those handling the affairs of a person who has died can choose how to handle medical deductions for optimum tax savings.

Benefit

Payments of medical expenses for a deceased spouse or dependent can be deducted as a medical expense in the year they are paid, even if this is before or after the person's death.

A decedent's personal representative (executor, administrator, etc.) has a choice of how to treat medical expenses— as an itemized deduction on the decedent's final income tax return (to the extent provided) or as a deduction on the estate tax return. Of course, if the decedent's estate is too small to require the filing of an estate tax return, there is no real choice; the deduction should automatically be treated as a deduction on the decedent's income tax return.

If the personal representative of a decedent's estate pays medical expenses within one year of death, an election can be made to treat the expenses as if they were paid by the decedent in the year the services were provided rather than the year in which they were paid. This may entitle the personal representative to file an amended return for the decedent for a prior year.

Example

In 2007, the decedent received treatment for a condition that eventually resulted in her death on May 1, 2008. At the time of death, payment for this treatment was outstanding. Assuming her personal representative pays any of her unreimbursed cost in February 2009, the personal representative may file an amended return for the decedent for 2007 to include the payment along with the decedent's other deductible medical expenses.

Condition

The decision on when and where to claim the decedent's medical expenses is made by the personal representative—the executor, administrator, or other person empowered by a court to act for the estate. This person can override a decision by a surviving spouse.

Planning Tip

Generally, if the decedent leaves an estate large enough to be subject to estate tax, it usually is preferable to claim the deduction on the estate tax return. The top estate tax rate in 2008 is 45 percent compared with a top individual income tax rate of only 35 percent. What's more, *all* of the medical expenses can be deducted on the estate tax return; there is no 7.5 percent floor for this purpose.

Pitfall

If the personal representative opts to deduct medical expenses on the decedent's income tax return, the 7.5 percent portion that is not deductible cannot be claimed on the estate tax return.

EXAMPLES OF NONDEDUCTIBLE EXPENSES FOR A DECEDENT

Burial fees.

Cremation costs.

Funeral expenses.

Perpetual care for a grave or mausoleum.

Where to Claim the Benefit

If the personal representative opts to deduct the medical expenses on the decedent's income tax return, a statement must be attached to the return agreeing *not* to claim the expenses as a deduction on the decedent's estate tax return.

CHAPTER 3

Education Costs

No one doubts the importance of education—for ourselves, our children, and our grandchildren—but obtaining it can be pricey. According to the College Board, the average cost of one year in a private college today is over $38,400 (most of the top schools are about $45,000 annually), and the cost of higher education is increasing at about 5 percent annually (compared with an overall inflation rate of about 3 percent). Fortunately, the tax law provides many incentives to help you save for education and to pay for it on a tax-advantaged basis.

This chapter explains education-related tax benefits, including:

- Employer-paid courses
- Scholarships, fellowships, and grants

- Hope credit
- Lifetime learning credit
- Job-related education
- Tuition and fees deduction
- Student loan interest
- Interest on U.S. savings bonds
- Coverdell education savings accounts (ESAs)
- Qualified tuition programs (529 plans)
- Seminars
- Educational travel
- Cancellation of a student loan
- Penalty-free withdrawals from IRAs

For more information, see IRS Publication 970, *Tax Benefits for Education*.

Employer-Paid Courses

Companies want an educated workforce. Some are willing to underwrite the cost of additional education for their employees. The tax law not only allows companies to deduct the costs they pay on behalf of workers for higher education, but also workers can enjoy this fringe benefit tax free up to a set dollar amount each year.

Benefit ⊗

If your employer pays or reimburses you for the cost of higher education, you are not taxed on payments up to $5,250 annually. If the courses are job-related, there is no dollar limit to the exclusion from income for this employer-paid fringe benefit. This fringe benefit is not subject to Social Security and Medicare (FICA) taxes.

If you work for an educational institution and receive tuition reductions, such benefit may be excludable (see Conditions, next).

Conditions

Different conditions apply to employer-paid education under an education assistance plan and tuition reduction if you work for a college or university.

EMPLOYER-PAID EDUCATION

Employer-paid education must be furnished under an employer's education assistance plan that does not discriminate in favor of owners or highly paid employees.

The courses need *not* be job-related to qualify for the limited exclusion of $5,250 annually. For example, if you are currently a programmer and your employer pays for accounting courses, you can still exclude the benefit.

There is no dollar limit on the amount you can exclude from income if you meet the following three conditions:

1. The courses relate to your current job.
2. The courses do not qualify you for a new profession.
3. You have already met the job's minimum education standards.

For example, if you are a programmer who takes more programming courses, the value of this benefit is fully excludable.

TUITION REDUCTION

If you work for an educational institution, you are not taxed on tuition reductions for you, your spouse, and your dependents (as well as widows or widowers of deceased or former employees) if:

- The courses are undergraduate courses. However, if you are a graduate student who is a teaching or research assistant, you aren't taxed on tuition reduction as long as it is in addition to regular pay for your teaching or research activities.
- The benefit is *not* payment for teaching or other services. However, if you receive a scholarship under the National Health Services Corps Scholarship Program or the Armed Forces Health Professionals Scholarship Program, you can exclude any reduction despite your service requirements.

If you are eligible for tuition reduction, the benefit is not limited to courses taken at the school in which you work. You can exclude from your income the value of courses you take at any school covered by a tuition reduction agreement (area colleges and universities typically have reciprocal class agreements).

Planning Tip

If you are seeking a job and plan to pursue college or graduate courses while working, look for a company with an educational assistance plan. The value of this benefit can be substantial to you if you use it fully and should be factored into the salary being offered for the position.

Example

You are in the 28 percent tax bracket and in 2008 your employer pays for courses totaling $5,000. If you had to pay for these courses yourself, you would need to earn an additional $6,944 in income to have the funds to pay for the courses yourself (assuming you can't deduct them).

Pitfalls

Generally, you must attain a certain course grade for your employer to pay for the education. Make sure you understand what you must do to obtain reimbursement or have your course fully paid by your employer.

You cannot use any benefit received under an employer's plan as the basis for claiming a second tax benefit. For example, if your employer pays $2,000 for a course you take, you cannot claim an education credit for this amount.

Where to Claim the Exclusion

If employer-provided education is excludable from income, it is not reported on your return. You may find the amount of employer-paid education benefits reported on your Form W-2 for information purposes only; it is not added to your compensation.

Scholarships, Fellowships, and Grants

There are over 20 million scholarships worth more than $1 trillion available each year. This money is available through government programs, nonprofit organizations, and corporations that support education. Grants are made on the basis of need, scholastics, or special talents (such as athletics or music). The tax law enables you to receive this money on a tax-free basis under certain circumstances.

Benefit ⊗

If you are enrolled in a degree program at a school and receive a scholarship, fellowship, or grant, you can exclude the portion of the grant for tuition, course-related fees, books, supplies, and equipment. There is no dollar limit on this exclusion.

If you receive a Fulbright award, it is fully taxable (unless you can claim the foreign earned income exclusion).

Condition

For tax-free treatment to apply, the grant must be for study in a degree program. A degree program includes:

- Primary and secondary school
- College or university degree programs
- Full-time or part-time scholarships for study at a school that provides an education program acceptable for full-time credit toward a degree or offers a program of training to prepare students for employment in a recognized occupation

Planning Tip

For education planning purposes, obtaining a scholarship, fellowship, or grant is the best way to finance learning. The award doesn't cost you anything and doesn't have to be repaid. Explore carefully any grants to which you, a spouse, or a dependent may be entitled.

Pitfalls

Scholarship amounts for room, board, and incidental expenses are taxable.

If you are a graduate student who receives payment (a stipend) for teaching, doing research, or providing other services as a condition of the grant, you are taxed on the payment. Such amount is reported on Form W-2 and is subject to income tax withholding.

Generally, no exclusion can be claimed if receipt of a federal grant is conditioned on your performing services in the future. For example, if you receive a scholarship that requires you to teach for at least three years as a condition of the grant, you cannot exclude this grant from your income.

Where to Claim the Exclusion

If the grant is excludable from income, you do not have to report it on your return.

If the grant is partially taxable (for example, you are not a degree candidate and so are taxed on the portion of the grant for housing), you report this as other income in the "Income" section of Form 1040 or Form 1040A. If you are a graduate student receiving a stipend for services, such amounts are reported as wages on your return, regardless of which type of return you file.

Hope Credit

The tax law allows you to claim a limited tax credit, called the Hope credit, when you pay for higher education. The credit applies whether you pay out-of-pocket from savings or borrow the money. You may claim the credit each year you qualify for it.

Benefit ⊗

There are two tax credits related to higher education expenses: the Hope credit and the lifetime learning credit. If you meet certain conditions, you can claim the Hope credit for higher education costs of up to $1,800 per student (100 percent of the first $1,200 of costs, plus 50 percent of the next $1,200 of costs). Thus, for example, if you have twins who are freshmen in college, you can qualify for a credit of up to $3,600.

Conditions

To claim the Hope credit, you must meet all five of these conditions:

1. Payments relate to the first two years of higher education.
2. Payments are made on behalf of an eligible student.
3. Payments are made to an eligible institution.
4. Payments cover qualified higher education costs.
5. Your modified adjusted gross income is not above a set limit.

FIRST TWO YEARS OF HIGHER EDUCATION

The credit applies for only the first two years of college or other postsecondary school. In effect, you can claim the credit only twice for the same student—for year one and for year two. This is so even if the student has not completed two full years (as measured by credits required for such completion).

Example

Your child starts college in September 2007, attending both the fall and spring semesters. Your child again enrolls in September 2008 for the fall and spring semesters. You may claim a credit for 2008 based on tuition for the spring semester of your child's freshman year and the fall semester of his sophomore year (a full year). You cannot claim the Hope credit for tuition paid for the spring semester in 2009.

ELIGIBLE STUDENT

The credit may be claimed for you, your spouse, or your dependent for whom you claim an exemption on your return. The student must be enrolled for at least one academic period (a semester, trimester, or quarter) during the year.

No credit may be claimed if the student has a federal or state felony drug conviction on his or her record.

ELIGIBLE EDUCATIONAL INSTITUTION

Only payments to an eligible institution entitle you to claim the credit. This includes any accredited public, nonprofit, or proprietary postsecondary institution eligible to participate in the student aid programs administered by the U.S. Department of Education. Ask your school if it is eligible, or check www.studentaid.ed.gov.

Enrollment must lead to a degree, certificate, or other recognized educational credential.

QUALIFIED HIGHER EDUCATION COSTS

Qualified expenses include *only* tuition and related fees. Related fees can include, for example, a student activity fee paid to the institution if it is required for all students and no portion of it covers personal expenses. Hobby or sports courses and noncredit courses do not qualify for the credit *unless* they are part of the student's degree program.

The following costs do *not* qualify for the credit:

- Room and board (even if they are required to be paid to the institution as a condition of enrollment)
- Books and supplies (unless they are required to be purchased directly from the institution)
- Medical expenses
- Transportation
- Insurance
- Personal living expenses

As a practical matter, the institution furnishes the student with an information return showing the payment of qualified tuition and related expenses for the year. The return, Form 1098-T, Tuition Payments Statement, for 2008 is issued by January 31, 2009.

If you prepay expenses for an academic period that begins within the first three months of 2009, you can include this amount when figuring your 2008 credit.

Example

In December 2008 you pay tuition for your child for the semester beginning February 2009. You can include the tuition payment as part of qualified expenses in figuring your 2008 credit.

MAGI LIMIT

The ability to claim the credit depends on your modified adjusted gross income (MAGI). MAGI for this purpose is adjusted gross income increased by the foreign earned income exclusion and other foreign items.

If your MAGI is below a phaseout range, then the full credit can be claimed; a partial credit is allowed for those with MAGI within the range. No credit can be claimed if MAGI exceeds the range. The phaseout range is adjusted annually for inflation. Table 3.1 shows the phaseout ranges for 2008.

TABLE 3.1 2008 MAGI Phaseout Range for Hope Credit

Filing Status	MAGI
Married filing jointly	$96,000–116,000
Other filing status*	$48,000–58,000

*No credit may be claimed for married filing separately.

Example

In 2008, you are single, with MAGI of $53,000. Your top credit is limited to $900 (one half of the maximum credit of $1,800), since you are midway in the MAGI phaseout range. If your MAGI is $40,000, you can claim a credit up to $1,800; if your MAGI is over $58,000, you cannot claim any credit.

Planning Tips

You can claim the credit even though eligible expenses are paid with the proceeds of a loan. You can also claim the credit if eligible expenses are paid by someone other than you, your spouse, or your dependent, such as the student's grandparent. The payment is treated as having been made by the student, and as your dependent, this entitles you to claim the credit if you are otherwise eligible to do so.

As the parent, if you pay the expenses but your MAGI is too high to permit you to claim the credit, you can waive your right to do so. This will allow your child to claim the credit on his or her own return (assuming the child has tax liability and can benefit from the credit). Your child can claim the credit even though you pay the expenses.

To allow your child to claim the credit you must forgo the dependency exemption for your child. To make the waiver, you do not have to file any special waiver forms or attach any statements to your return or to the child's return.

If your child cannot use the credit, consider taking the above-the-line deduction for tuition and fees if you are qualified to do so (explained later in this chapter). The tuition and fees deduction has a higher MAGI limit so you may qualify for this benefit even though your MAGI prevents you from claiming the credit.

Pitfalls

The credit must be coordinated with other education tax benefits you may be qualified to use. You can claim the credit in the same year in which you receive distributions from a Coverdell education savings account (ESA) or 529 plan. However, the expenses on which you base the credit cannot be the same expenses used to figure the tax-free portion of the distributions.

Example

Your child's college tuition bill for the year is $15,000. You pay $5,000 of this amount from a 529 plan. For purposes of figuring the credit, you can only take $10,000 of eligible expenses into account ($5,000 is used as a tax-free distribution from the 529 plan).

If you claim a credit and in a later year (after you have filed the return and claimed the credit) receive a refund of an amount that was used to figure the credit, you must recapture some or all of the credit. This means you must repay some or all of the credit. You treat the recaptured amount as additional tax liability for the year of recapture. Do not amend the return on which the credit was claimed.

Example

In 2008, you take a Hope credit of $1,800 based on $2,500 of tuition costs. In 2009, your child receives a grant reimbursing him for tuition of $1,000. You must recapture $500 (50 percent of $1,000). You report this recapture as "other income" on your 2009 return.

You may not claim the Hope credit if you claim an above-the-line deduction for tuition and fees for a student (discussed later in this chapter). You must choose which write-off gives you the greater benefit, assuming you qualify for each.

Example

You are a single parent with MAGI in 2008 of $40,000 and pay $5,000 in tuition for your child. You can claim a Hope credit of $1,800, which gives you a tax savings of $1,800. Or you can claim an above-the-line deduction for tuition of $4,000, which gives you a tax savings of $1,000 if you are in the 25 percent tax bracket ($4,000 × 25%). In this case, you'd choose the credit alternative.

You cannot claim the credit for expenses that are paid by tax-free scholarships, fellowships, grants, veterans' educational assistance, or employer-provided educational assistance.

Where to Claim the Credit

The Hope credit is figured on Form 8863, Education Credits. The credit is then entered in the "Tax and Credits" section of Form 1040, or in the "Tax, Credits, and Payments" section of Form 1040A.

You may not claim the credit if you file Form 1040EZ.

Lifetime Learning Credit

The tax law allows you to claim a limited tax credit, called the lifetime learning credit, when you pay for higher education. The credit applies whether you pay out-of-pocket from savings or borrow the money. You may claim the credit each year you qualify for it.

Benefit ⊗

If certain conditions are met, you can claim a credit of up to $2,000 on your return for the payment of qualified higher education costs for you, your spouse, or your dependent. In contrast to the Hope credit, which is a per student credit, the lifetime learning credit is per taxpayer. So if you have three children in college, your lifetime learning credit for the year is limited to $2,000 (assuming you qualify to claim it).

Unlike the Hope credit, which applies only for the first two years of higher education, the lifetime learning credit can be claimed for any higher education, including graduate-level courses.

Conditions

Most of the conditions for the lifetime learning credit are the same as those for the Hope credit detailed earlier, unless otherwise noted here. Thus, the same MAGI limits apply to the lifetime learning credit, and the same planning tips and pitfalls also apply.

ELIGIBLE STUDENT

There is no ban on claiming the lifetime learning credit for a student who has a felony drug conviction on his or her record, as there is for claiming the Hope credit.

HIGHER EDUCATION

Unlike the Hope credit, which can be claimed only for courses leading to a degree, the lifetime learning credit can be claimed for one or more courses at an eligible educational institution that are part of a postsecondary degree program or part of a nondegree program taken to acquire or improve job skills. In other words, the student does not need to be pursuing a degree or other recognized educational credential.

There is no limit on the number of years for which the lifetime learning credit may be claimed.

Planning Tip

Since the lifetime learning credit cannot be claimed for a student for whom a Hope credit is claimed, decide which credit produces the greater tax savings. As a general rule, assuming that either credit could be claimed, you will probably be better off taking the lifetime learning credit if qualifying expenses exceed $7,500; if expenses are below this amount, then the Hope credit may be the better choice.

Pitfalls

The same pitfalls applicable to the Hope credit apply to the lifetime learning credit.

Where to Claim the Credit

The lifetime learning credit is figured on Form 8863, Education Credits. The credit is then entered in the "Tax and Credits" section of Form 1040, or in the "Tax, Credits, and Payments" section of Form 1040A. You may not claim the credit if you file Form 1040EZ.

Job-Related Education

Americans are always trying to better themselves. Whether you are a teacher taking courses toward an advanced degree or a data processor learning the latest technology, you may be eligible to deduct your education costs.

Benefit ⬚

If you pay for education related to your current line of work, you may be able to deduct your expenses.

If you qualify for the deduction by meeting all of the conditions, you claim the deduction as a miscellaneous itemized deduction if you are an employee or as a business expense if you are self-employed. This means that if you are an employee, you can take the deduction only if your miscellaneous itemized deductions exceed 2 percent of your adjusted gross income. There is no dollar limit on this deduction.

Conditions

To deduct education expenses, you must meet all five of these conditions:

1. You are an employee or self-employed.
2. You already meet the minimum job requirements for your work (as set by your employer or state law).

3. The courses maintain or improve your skills or you are required by your employer or by law to take the course to keep your current salary or position.

4. The courses do not lead to a new line of work.

5. You pay for eligible education expenses.

EMPLOYED OR SELF-EMPLOYED

You cannot deduct the cost of courses taken before you start to work.

MINIMUM JOB REQUIREMENTS

Minimum job requirements are based on a review of your employer's standards, the laws and regulations of your state, and the standards of your profession or business. Just because you are currently employed doesn't automatically mean you meet minimum job requirements. You may be hired provisionally on the condition that you complete certain courses.

If job requirements change after you enter the job market or profession, any courses you take to meet the new standards are deductible.

Example

You graduated from college with a degree in physical therapy and start to work in your chosen occupation. Then state law is changed to require physical therapists to complete at least one year of graduate school to retain certification. You can deduct the cost of the additional year of schooling because you had already met your initial minimum job requirements.

MAINTAIN OR IMPROVE SKILLS OR REQUIRED BY EMPLOYER OR BY LAW

General education courses are not deductible. The courses must be designed to keep you up-to-date and qualified.

Courses that give you a specialty *within* your current line of work are deductible.

EXAMPLES OF DEDUCTIBLE COURSES

- Attorney in practice who takes LLM courses to obtain a master's degree in taxation.
- Continuing education courses by professionals.
- Dentist who takes courses in orthodontics. This post-graduate schooling improves professional skills as a dentist.
- Practicing psychiatrist who takes courses at an accredited psychoanalytic institution.
- Psychiatrist who takes personal therapy sessions.
- Salesperson who is encouraged by his or her employer to pursue an MBA degree in order to move up in the company because the degree merely enhances his skills.
- Teachers may deduct courses taken for job changes within the teaching profession (e.g., elementary to secondary school, one classroom subject to another, classroom teacher to guidance counselor, and classroom teacher to principal).

NOT A NEW LINE OF WORK

If the courses enable you to follow a new line of work, they are not deductible.

EXAMPLES OF NONDEDUCTIBLE COURSES

- Law school (even by someone who intends to continue in his or her original line of work, such as accounting).
- Nurse who takes courses that qualify him to become a physician's assistant.
- NASA engineer who obtained a pilot's license (even though this helped with his engineering activities).

ELIGIBLE EDUCATION EXPENSES

If you qualify for the deduction, it is not limited to the cost of tuition and fees as is the case with many other types of education tax breaks. The deduction applies not only to the cost of courses but also to:

- Books and supplies.
- Local transportation expenses to and from the course, including bus, subway, or train fares. If you use your car, you can deduct mileage at the rate of 48.5 cents per mile, plus parking and tolls.
- Lodging, meals, and transportation. If you attend courses out of town, you can deduct away-from-home expenses. The deduction for meals is limited to 50 percent of actual cost.

Planning Tip

Check to see whether education expenses qualify for an education credit or the above-the-line tuition and fees deduction, which may provide a greater tax benefit than an itemized deduction subject to the 2 percent floor.

Pitfalls

As a practical matter, even if your costs for taking courses are eligible for the deduction, you may not achieve any meaningful tax benefit from claiming them. First, as mentioned earlier, the deduction is limited to amounts exceeding 2 percent of your adjusted gross income. Thus, if your AGI is $50,000, your total miscellaneous itemized deductions must exceed $1,000 to claim any write-off; you lose the first $1,000 of deductions.

Second, claiming miscellaneous itemized deductions can trigger or increase the alternative minimum tax (AMT). The reason: Miscellaneous itemized deductions are *not* deductible for AMT purposes.

Where to Claim the Deduction

You must file Form 1040 to claim the deduction; you cannot claim the deduction if you file Form 1040A or 1040EZ.

If you are an employee, you complete Form 2106, Employee Business Expenses, or 2106-EZ, Unreimbursed Employee Business Expenses, to figure your unreimbursed employee expenses that are then deducted on Schedule A.

If you are self-employed, you deduct the expenses directly as a business expense on Schedule C.

Tuition and Fees Deduction

The tax law allows you to claim a limited deduction when you pay for higher education. The deduction applies whether you pay out-of-pocket from savings or borrow the money. You may claim the deduction each year you qualify for it. The deduction expires at the end of 2009, unless Congress extends it.

Benefit ①

If you pay tuition and fees for higher education for you, your spouse, or a dependent, you may be able to deduct up to $4,000 in 2008 as an adjustment to gross income, even if you don't itemize your other deductions.

Conditions

To claim the deduction for tuition and fees, you must meet all five of these conditions:

1. Be an eligible taxpayer.
2. Make payments to an eligible educational institution.
3. Pay qualified expenses.
4. Have MAGI below a set amount.
5. You do not claim an education credit.

ELIGIBLE TAXPAYER

You can claim the deduction for you, your spouse, or your dependent for whom you claim an exemption on your return.

You may not claim the deduction if you are married filing separately. You may not claim the deduction if you can be claimed as a dependent on another taxpayer's return.

ELIGIBLE EDUCATIONAL INSTITUTION

Only tuition and fees paid to an eligible educational institution qualify for the deduction. An eligible educational institution includes any college, university, vocational school, or postsecondary institution eligible to participate in the financial aid programs of the U.S. Department of Education.

QUALIFIED EXPENSES

The same expenses that qualify for the Hope credit discussed earlier qualify for the tuition and fees deduction. Student activity fees and even the cost of books can be treated as deductible fees if the cost is paid to the eligible educational institution. As a practical matter, the institution furnishes the student with an information return showing the payment of qualified tuition and related expenses for the year. The return, Form 1098-T, Tuition Payments Statement, for 2008 is issued by January 31, 2009.

Qualified expenses do not include any amounts paid by tax-free scholarships, tax-free distributions from Coverdell education savings accounts or 529 plans, and excludable interest from the redemption of U.S. savings bonds.

Qualified expenses paid directly to the educational institution under a court-approved divorce decree are treated as paid by the student (not by the person making the payments), so only the student is eligible to claim the deduction. Remember that the student can claim the deduction only if he or she cannot be claimed as the dependent of another taxpayer.

The same treatment applies to qualified expenses paid by someone else (such as a grandparent). Again, the student is treated as making the payment, and the student is eligible to claim the deduction only if he or she cannot be claimed as the dependent of another taxpayer.

MAGI LIMIT

You can claim the deduction only if your MAGI is no more than the limit found in Table 3.2. MAGI for this purpose is adjusted gross income increased by the foreign earned

TABLE 3.2 2008 MAGI Limits for Tuition Deduction

Filing Status*	MAGI Limit for $4,000 Deduction	MAGI Limit for $2,000 Deduction
Married filing jointly	Not more than $130,000	More than $130,000 but not more than $160,000
Other taxpayers	Not more than $65,000	More than $65,000 but not more than $80,000

*You cannot claim the deduction if you are married filing separately.

income exclusion, income from Puerto Rico or American Samoa, and the foreign housing exclusion or deduction.

Example

You are married and file a joint return with your spouse. If your MAGI is:

- No more than $130,000, your deduction is $4,000.
- More than $130,000 but not more than $160,000, your deduction is $2,000.
- Over $160,000, your deduction is zero.

NO EDUCATION CREDIT

You cannot claim the deduction for a student's expenses for which you claim a Hope credit or lifetime learning credit (education credits). If you qualify for both the tuition and fees deduction and an education credit, you must choose the write-off that provides the greater benefit; generally this will be a credit.

Planning Tip

Compare the tax savings from claiming the deduction with the savings from an education credit. Remember that the amount of a credit equals the amount of your tax savings from claiming it. Usually the tax credit provides the greater benefit. Use the following worksheet to compare your tax savings:

Tuition and Fees Deduction		Education Credit	
Amount of deduction	$_____	Amount of credit	$_____
× your tax bracket	$_____		
Tax savings	$_____	Tax savings	$_____

Example

You are single and your MAGI permits you to claim either a $4,000 tuition and fees deduction or a $2,000 lifetime learning credit. You are in the 25 percent tax bracket. The deduction provides you with a $1,000 tax savings ($4,000 × 25%). The credit provides you with a $2,000 tax savings. But if your MAGI limited your lifetime learning credit to less than $1,000 (e.g., your MAGI is $50,000), you would reap a greater tax savings by claiming the deduction.

Pitfall

Even one dollar over the MAGI limit prevents you from claiming a deduction. There is no phaseout of this deduction, as there is with many other deductions.

Where to Claim the Deduction

Figure the amount of the deduction on Form 8917, Tuition and Fees Deduction. Then enter the deduction on Form 1040 or 1040A in the section called "Adjusted Gross Income." You cannot claim the deduction if you file Form 1040EZ.

Student Loan Interest

Millions of students must borrow money to pay for their education. Repayment of student loans runs between 5 and 30 years. Fortunately, the tax law allows interest on student loans to be deductible each year within limits.

Benefit ⬆

If you pay interest on student loans, you may be able to deduct up to $2,500 of interest as an adjustment to gross income (if your actual interest payment is more than $2,500, your deduction is limited to that amount). There is no limit on the number of years you can claim this deduction; as long as you continue to pay off the loan, you can deduct your interest if eligible to do so.

If the loan is canceled, you may qualify for tax-free treatment on the debt forgiveness (explained later in this chapter).

Conditions

There are a couple of conditions for claiming a deduction for student loan interest as an adjustment to gross income. You must meet both:

1. The loan must be a qualified loan.
2. Your modified adjusted gross income cannot exceed a set limit (there is a partial deduction allowed if MAGI falls within a phaseout range).

LOAN QUALIFICATIONS

To be treated as a student loan for which interest is deductible, the loan must have been taken out solely to pay qualified education expenses. Qualified education expenses relate to a qualified educational institution (virtually all accredited public, nonpublic, and proprietary postsecondary institutions are eligible educational institutions). Qualified education expenses include:

- Tuition and fees.
- Room and board.
- Books, supplies, and equipment.
- Other necessary expenses (including transportation to and from school).

You cannot deduct interest on a loan from a related person or made under a qualified employer plan. Related persons include:

- Spouses.
- Siblings and half-siblings.
- Parents.
- Grandparents.
- Children.
- Grandchildren.
- Certain corporations, partnerships, trusts, and exempt organizations.

The loan must be for you, your spouse, or your dependent (in the year you take out the loan). The loan must be taken for an eligible student, who is enrolled at least half-time in a degree program.

You must be legally obligated to make payments on the loan. For example, if your child took out the loan and you are now helping her make the payments, you cannot deduct the interest because you are not the borrower (you are not legally responsible for the loan).

If the loan is a revolving line of credit (e.g., credit card debt), interest qualifies as student loan interest only if funds on the line are used solely to pay qualified education expenses.

MAGI LIMITS

You can claim the full deduction if your modified adjusted gross income is below the phaseout range. A partial deduction is permitted if your MAGI is within the phaseout range. No

TABLE 3.3 2008 Phaseout Ranges for Student Interest
Deduction

Filing Status*	MAGI
Unmarried (single), head of household, and surviving widow(er)	$ 55,000–70,000
Married filing jointly	$115,000–145,000

*You cannot claim the deduction if you are married filing separately.

deduction can be claimed if your MAGI exceeds the phaseout
range, which is adjusted annually for inflation. Table 3.3
shows the 2008 phaseout ranges for claiming the student
interest deduction.

Example

You are single and graduated from college in May
2008. You start to pay back your loans, paying
interest in 2008 of $800. You can deduct this amount
in full if your MAGI is under $55,000. If, however,
you landed your dream job and earned $72,000 in
just seven months remaining in 2008, you cannot
deduct any of your student loan interest because your
MAGI is above the limit for your filing status.

Planning Tip

In some instances, the cancellation of student loans can be
tax free (usually the cancellation of debt is taxable). This is
explained later in this chapter.

Pitfall

You cannot claim a double benefit for the same interest deduction. For example, if you take out a home equity loan to pay your child's college expenses, you cannot claim a student interest deduction if you deduct the mortgage interest as an itemized deduction. It is, of course, more favorable to treat the interest as student loan interest to the extent possible.

Where to Claim the Deduction

The deduction is claimed on Form 1040 or 1040A in the section called "Adjusted Gross Income." No special form or schedule is required. However, you can use a worksheet in the instructions to your return to figure your allowable deduction if your MAGI falls within the phaseout range.

You cannot claim the deduction if you file Form 1040EZ.

Interest on U.S. Savings Bonds

The first savings bonds, series A, were issued in 1935 at 75 percent of face value in denominations of $25 to $1,000, paying 2.9 percent accrued interest, and were sold through the U.S. Post Office. Since then savings bonds have become a permanent investment vehicle. Americans purchase an average of $8 million in U.S. savings bonds per week. If you happen to be holding these bonds and decide to cash them in to pay for higher education costs, you may be eligible to receive the interest tax free.

Benefit ⊗

If you redeem U.S. savings bonds to pay for qualified higher education costs or to contribute to a 529 plan or Coverdell education savings account, you are not taxed on the interest as long as your modified adjusted gross income is below a set amount. There is no dollar limit to this benefit; if you qualify you can exclude from income all of the interest received on the redemption of the bonds.

Conditions

Assuming you have not been reporting interest on the savings bonds annually but deferring it, you can claim the exclusion if you meet all four of these conditions:

1. Eligible bonds.
2. Eligible taxpayer.
3. MAGI limit.
4. Qualified use of redemption proceeds.

ELIGIBLE BONDS

The exclusion applies only to series EE bonds issued after 1989 or series I bonds. You cannot claim the exclusion when redeeming older EE bonds or E bonds.

ELIGIBLE TAXPAYER

You must be the purchaser of the bond and hold it in your name or the joint name of you and your spouse. You must have been at least 24 years old when you purchased the bonds.

No exclusion can be claimed for interest on bonds held in the child's name or in the joint name of you and your child.

If you are married, you must file jointly to claim the exclusion.

TABLE 3.4 2008 Phaseout Ranges for Savings Bond Interest Exclusion

Filing Status	MAGI
Unmarried (single) and head of household	$ 67,100–82,100
Married filing jointly and surviving widow(er)	$100,650–130,650

MAGI LIMIT

To claim a full or partial exclusion you cannot have modified adjusted gross income (MAGI) over a fixed dollar limit (which is adjusted annually for inflation). MAGI for this purpose means AGI increased by the redeemed interest, the deductions for tuition and fees and for student loan interest, foreign earned income exclusion and other foreign items, and the exclusion for employer-paid adoption.

Table 3.4 shows the phaseout range for 2008. If your MAGI is below the start of the phaseout range, you can claim a full exclusion. If your MAGI is over the phaseout range, no exclusion can be claimed, even if all of the other conditions are met. If your MAGI is within the phaseout range, you can claim a partial exclusion.

Example

In 2008, you are married filing jointly with MAGI of $115,650. You redeem bonds with interest of $5,000, and you use all of the redemption proceeds for qualified higher education expenses. You can exclude $2,500 of the $5,000 interest because your MAGI is in the middle of the phaseout range.

QUALIFIED USE OF REDEMPTION PROCEEDS

The proceeds must be used only for a qualified purpose:

- Paying higher education costs (tuition and fees for a college, university, or vocational school that meets federal financial aid standards). The higher education expenses can be for you, your spouse, or a dependent.
- Funding a 529 plan or a Coverdell education savings account.

If the proceeds from the redemption exceed the amount used for a qualified purpose, you can exclude a portion of the interest based on the ratio of expenses (or funding) to the redemption amount.

Example

In 2008, you redeem bonds worth $10,000, using $5,000 to pay your child's qualified higher education costs. Interest on the bonds is $3,000. Since half of the proceeds were used for qualified expenses, half of the interest, or $1,500, is eligible for the exclusion (assuming the other conditions are met).

Planning Tips

If you are holding EE or I savings bonds and want to know how much they are worth today, you can check their redemption values at www.savingsbonds.gov.

The U.S. Treasury has changed the way in which interest on Series EE bonds is computed. Rather than adjusting the interest semiannually, these bonds now pay a fixed rate until redemption or maturity. As a result, Series I bonds may be a better option because their interest rate still adjusts semiannually for inflation.

Pitfalls

You cannot use this exclusion to pay college expenses for your grandchild *unless* the grandchild is your dependent in the year in which the bonds are redeemed.

You cannot claim the exclusion if you are married and file a separate return from your spouse.

Where to Claim the Exclusion

If you claim the exclusion, you must complete Form 8815, Exclusion of Interest from Series EE and I Bonds Issued after 1989, and attach it to your return.

Coverdell Education Savings Accounts

Is the high cost of a prep school or college in your child or grandchild's future? If you decide to help save for this expense, consider doing so using a tax-advantaged savings account, called a Coverdell education savings account (ESA), designed for this purpose.

Benefit ⊗

You may be able to contribute up to $2,000 annually to a savings account for each beneficiary. The account is called a Coverdell education savings account (ESA) (it used to be called an education IRA). The account can have multiple contributors, but no more than $2,000 can be placed in the account for any one year.

Earnings on contributions accumulate tax deferred. If withdrawals from the account are used to pay qualified education expenses, the earnings become tax free.

Conditions

There are a couple of conditions for funding a Coverdell education savings account as well as for taking tax-free distributions.

1. For purposes of contributions, they can be made only on behalf of an eligible beneficiary (defined next) by a contributor whose modified adjusted gross income does not exceed set limits. Contributions must be made in cash, not property.

2. For purposes of tax-free distributions, funds must be used only for eligible expenses.

ELIGIBLE BENEFICIARY

Generally, a beneficiary is a person who is under the age of 18 at the time the contribution is made. Thus, for example, if a beneficiary attains the age of 18 on July 1, 2008, contributions can be made through June 30, 2008.

A beneficiary can also be a special needs person over the age of 18. A special needs beneficiary is one who requires additional time to complete his or her education because of a physical, mental, or emotional condition. This would include, for example, a person with a learning disability.

MAGI FOR CONTRIBUTORS

There is no familial requirement for contributors. Anyone can make a Coverdell education savings account contribution on behalf of an eligible beneficiary, as long as the contributor meets MAGI limits. Contributions can even be made by the beneficiary herself.

In order to contribute the full $2,000 to a Coverdell education savings account, your modified adjusted gross income cannot be more than a set limit. MAGI for this purpose means adjusted gross income increased by the foreign earned income exclusion, the foreign housing exclusion or deduction, the exclusion for income from American Samoa, or the exclusion for income from Puerto Rico.

A reduced contribution limit applies if your MAGI falls within a phaseout range. No contribution can be made if your MAGI exceeds the phaseout range, which is adjusted annually for inflation. The MAGI phaseout range for Coverdell ESA contributors in 2008 may be found in Table 3.5.

TABLE 3.5 2008 MAGI Phaseout Ranges for Coverdell ESA Contributors

Filing Status	MAGI Phaseout Range
Married filing jointly	$190,000–220,000
Other taxpayers	$ 95,000–110,000

Example

In 2008, you are a single parent with MAGI of $80,000. You can make a $2,000 contribution on behalf of your 12-year-old child. But if your MAGI is between $95,000 and $110,000, only part of the $2,000 may be contributed (you figure the limit using a worksheet provided in IRS Publication 970).

CASH CONTRIBUTIONS

Contributions must be made in cash; you cannot contribute property to a Coverdell ESA. If you own stocks or mutual funds, you must sell the property and invest the proceeds. You may incur a capital gain on the sale of property.

ELIGIBLE EXPENSES

Unlike most other education tax breaks that are restricted to higher education, Coverdell education savings accounts can be used for education in grades K–12 and/or for higher education. Primary and secondary school can be public, private, or religious school.

The range of eligible expenses for which tax-free withdrawals can be made is quite broad. Just about anything related to education is a qualified expense.

EXAMPLES OF ELIGIBLE ELEMENTARY AND SECONDARY SCHOOL EXPENSES

Academic tutoring

Books

Computer and peripheral equipment; software only if it is predominantly educational in nature

Extended day programs required or provided by the school

Internet access

Special services for a special needs beneficiary

Supplies

Transportation

Uniforms

EXAMPLES OF ELIGIBLE HIGHER EDUCATION EXPENSES

Books, supplies, and equipment

Room and board

Tuition and fees

Planning Tips

You can open a Coverdell education savings account at any bank or other financial institution that has received IRS approval to offer Coverdell ESAs. You can then select the investments you prefer, from certificates of deposit to stocks and mutual funds (to the extent available from the institution you select).

Just like IRA contributions, contributions to Coverdell ESAs can be made up to the due date of the return for the year to which they relate. However, obtaining a filing extension does not extend the deadline for making contributions.

Example

Contributions for 2008 may be made only up to April 15, 2009, even if the contributor and/or the beneficiary has obtained a six-month filing extension.

You can turn taxable custodial accounts into tax-free Coverdell education savings accounts by using the funds in the custodial account for contributions. However, only cash contributions are permitted to a Coverdell education savings account, so investments in the custodial accounts must first be sold so that the proceeds can be contributed.

Example

Junior has $5,000 in a custodial account that owns shares in a mutual fund, the earnings from which are reported annually as taxable income to Junior. He can opt to sell $2,000 from the mutual fund in his custodial account each year and contribute the proceeds to a Coverdell education savings account of which he is the designated beneficiary (assuming he meets the age and MAGI limits). The account can own shares in the same mutual fund, but now the earnings become tax deferred and, if funds are withdrawn for qualified expenses, they become tax free.

You can change accounts from one financial institution to another by means of a tax-free rollover. You may not be satisfied with the service or investment options you have at one financial institution and can switch by means of a rollover to another financial institution.

You can move money in a Coverdell ESA between certain beneficiaries on a tax-free basis. The amount withdrawn from a Coverdell ESA can be rolled over to the same or a new designated beneficiary who is a member of the original beneficiary's family (listed in the next section). The rollover must be completed within 60 days. There are no tax consequences to naming a new designated beneficiary (as long as such beneficiary is permissible).

You can fund contributions to a Coverdell ESA by means of a direct deposit of a tax refund. For example, say you are owed a refund on your 2008 return. Use the refund to contribute to a Coverdell ESA (assuming you meet eligibility requirements) by filing the return early enough for the IRS to process it and electronically transfer the refund to the Coverdell ESA by April 15, 2009, for a 2008 contribution (you can also use the 2008 tax refund to make a 2009 contribution).

Anyone who receives a military death gratuity or payment under the Servicemen's Group Life Insurance (SGLI) program can contribute this amount to a Coverdell ESA; the usual contribution limit and MAGI limit do not apply in this case.

Pitfalls

If you contribute more than $2,000 on behalf of a beneficiary within one year, the excess amount is subject to a 6 percent excise tax. The penalty is paid by the beneficiary (not the contributor). But the penalty can be avoided by withdrawing the excess contribution, plus any earnings on the contribution, before the beginning of the sixth month following the year of the contribution (e.g., by May 31, 2009, for 2008 contributions).

Example

In 2008, Aunt Mary contributes $2,000 to a Coverdell ESA for Amy. Unaware of Aunt Mary's contribution, Uncle Ed also contributes $2,000 to a Coverdell ESA for Amy in 2008. Amy can avoid the 6 percent excise tax on the excess $2,000 contribution by withdrawing it, plus any earnings, by May 31, 2009. (Whether she chooses to give it back to Aunt Mary or Uncle Ed or split it between them is up to Amy.)

The 6 percent excise tax continues to apply each year in which excess contributions (and earnings on excess contributions) remain in the Coverdell ESA.

Taxable distributions, which are withdrawals made to pay for noneligible expenses, are not only taxed as ordinary income but are subject to a 10 percent additional tax. However, the 10 percent penalty does not apply to distributions that meet any of these conditions:

- Distributions are made to a beneficiary or to the estate of a designated beneficiary on or after the death of a designated beneficiary.
- Distributions are made because the designated beneficiary is disabled.

- Distributions are made because the designated beneficiary received a tax-free grant or educational assistance allowance that equals or exceeds the distribution.
- Distributions are taxable only because the qualified expenses are reduced by expenses taken into account in figuring an education credit.

Withdrawals from a Coverdell ESA can be made in the same year in which an education credit is claimed. However, the same expenses cannot be used for both benefits.

Withdrawals from both a Coverdell ESA and a 529 plan are permitted in the same year. But if total withdrawals exceed qualified higher education expenses, the expenses must be allocated between the Coverdell ESA and 529 plan to figure the taxable portion of the withdrawals. Generally, the allocation is based on the ratio of the Coverdell ESA withdrawals to the total withdrawals.

Example

In 2008, Henry begins college and withdraws $800 from a Coverdell ESA and $3,200 from a 529 plan to pay $3,000 of eligible expenses. Of the $800 withdrawn, $600 is tax free: $800 Coverdell ESA withdrawal ÷ $4,000 total withdrawals = 0.2; 0.2 × $3,000 qualified expenses = $600.

Funds remaining in the account become taxable to the beneficiary within 30 days of attaining age 30 (or within 30 days of death if the beneficiary dies before age 30). The

30-year age limit does not apply to a special needs beneficiary (defined earlier).

However, tax on the earnings in the account can be avoided if the balance in the account is transferred to another eligible beneficiary within 60 days of attaining age 30 (or death if earlier). An eligible beneficiary for this purpose includes members of the beneficiary's family:

- Spouse
- Child or stepchild
- Grandchild
- Brother, sister, half-brother, or half-sister
- Niece or nephew
- Parent or stepparent
- Grandparent
- In-laws and the spouses of any of the listed relatives

Where to Claim the Exclusion

Contributions to a Coverdell education savings account are not reported on the return of the contributor or the beneficiary. Similarly, withdrawals that are not taxable are not reported on any return.

If contributions are subject to the 6 percent excise tax, the beneficiary figures the excise tax in Part V of Form 5329, Additional Taxes on Qualified Plans (Including IRAs) and Other Tax-Favored Accounts, and report it as "Other Taxes" on Form 1040.

If withdrawals from a Coverdell ESA are taxable, they are reported on the beneficiary's return as "other income" on the return on Form 1040 or in the "Income" section on Form 1040A. If they are also subject to the 10 percent additional tax, this amount is figured in Part II of Form 5329, Additional Taxes on Qualified Plans (Including IRAs) and Other Tax-Favored Accounts.

Qualified Tuition Programs (529 Plans)

You can help save for the higher education expenses of your child or grandchild using a tax-advantaged account called a 529 plan. The 529 plan is a qualified tuition program offering federal (and in some cases state) tax incentives for savings. Federal tax breaks for 529 plans, which had been scheduled to expire at the end of 2010, have been made permanent.

Benefit ⊗

There are two types of qualified tuition programs (QTPs): a prepayment plan under which payments are guaranteed to cover (or partially cover) tuition, regardless of tuition increases, and a savings-type plan in which the funds you will have available to pay for higher education depend on the investment performance of your account. From a tax perspective, however, both types of plans are governed by the same tax rules under Section 529 of the Internal Revenue Code (hence the name "529 plans"), and both types of plans have the same benefits and conditions.

While contributions to qualified tuition programs do not generate a federal income tax deduction or credit, the long-term benefits are considerable:

- Earnings within the plan are tax deferred.
- If funds in the plan are used to pay qualified higher education costs, they are tax free (the earnings on the contributions are never taxed in this case).

- Unused amounts can be transferred tax free to another beneficiary if the original beneficiary does not go to college or otherwise need the funds.

There may be state income tax breaks for the contributions to qualified tuition programs as well. For example, if you are a resident in New York, you can deduct contributions to the New York 529 College Savings Program up to $5,000 per taxpayer per year on your New York state income tax return.

Conditions

Most conditions and requirements are fixed by each state's own 529 plan. However, for tax purposes, there are a couple of key conditions to obtaining all of the benefits under a qualified tuition program.

1. Contributions can be made only to qualified tuition programs. There are no federal tax limits on annual or total contributions to a 529 plan. These limits are fixed by each state's unique program.
2. Distributions can be withdrawn only for qualified expenses.

QUALIFIED TUITION PROGRAMS

Contributions can be made only to state plans and IRS-approved private college/university plans. A personally devised plan, even one that mimics the investment strategies of the state plans, does not entitle you to these benefits.

At present, all states offer savings-type plans and nearly two dozen have prepaid tuition plans.

QUALIFIED EXPENSES

For distributions from qualified tuition programs to be tax free, they must be used only to pay for qualified expenses. These include tuition for higher education, fees, books, supplies, and room and board (if the student is enrolled at least half time).

There is no set dollar limit on these expenses, including room and board. Thus, any reasonable amount for room and board (including expenses of off-campus housing) can qualify.

Planning Tips

The terms and conditions of qualified tuition programs vary considerably from state to state. You can learn about the investment options, fees, and other rules on state 529 plans at www.savingforcollege.com. For details on the private 529 plan created by a consortium of private colleges and universities (about 275 schools now participate), go to www.independent529plan.org.

If you plan for your child to attend your alma mater on a legacy basis, ask the school whether it offers or plans to offer a tuition prepayment plan.

For purposes of the federal financial aid formula, funds in 529 plans are not considered to be the assets of the student.

Qualified tuition programs can be used effectively for estate planning purposes. For example, a wealthy grandparent can reduce the size of his or her estate while funding an education savings plan for a grandchild with little or no gift tax cost. If you plan to make sizable contributions in one year, you can elect to treat the contributions as made equally over five years. This will entitle you to apply the annual gift tax exclusion five times to avoid or reduce gift tax.

Example

In 2008, when the annual gift tax exclusion is $12,000 per beneficiary, you contribute $60,000 (or $120,000 per couple) to a state savings plan for your grandchild. Since you can treat the $60,000 as having been made ratably over five years, there is no taxable gift in this transfer. The transfer is fully offset by the annual gift tax exclusion ($12,000 × 5).

If the contribution exceeds this limit, the excess amount is treated as a gift in the year the contribution is made.

Amounts in a 529 plan can be transferred to a new beneficiary or rolled over tax free within 60 days of a distribution. There is a limit of one transfer or rollover per year. However, a beneficiary can be changed without making a transfer or rollover; the new name is substituted for the old one on the same account. This option applies only if the new beneficiary is a member of the old beneficiary's family, which includes:

- Child or grandchild.
- Stepson or stepdaughter.
- Sibling or stepsibling.
- Parent or grandparent.
- Stepparent.
- Aunt or uncle.

- Niece or nephew.
- Son-in-law, daughter-in-law, father-in-law, mother-in-law, brother-in-law, or sister-in-law.
- The spouse of any relative listed above.
- First cousin.

In the case of a savings-type 529 plan, if the account declines in value from the amount contributed, the loss can be recognized when all of the funds in the account are distributed. The IRS says that the loss is claimed as a miscellaneous itemized deduction on Schedule A of Form 1040, which is deductible to the extent total miscellaneous itemized deductions exceed 2 percent of adjusted gross income. Some tax experts believe that the loss is simply claimed as an ordinary loss. This theory has yet to be tested in court.

Funds within 529 plans offer asset protection in case of bankruptcy. Contributions to the plan made at least one year but less than two years before filing for bankruptcy are protected up to $5,000. Contributions made two years or more before filing for bankruptcy are fully protected (no dollar limit applies). Only contributions made within one year of filing for bankruptcy are at risk.

Pitfalls

If funds are withdrawn from a 529 plan and *not* used for qualified education expenses, earnings on the distribution are taxable. For example, if part of a distribution is used for spending money or travel expenses, the earnings on this portion of the distribution are taxable. The cost of a computer may or may not be a qualified education expense.

Example

If $25,000 is withdrawn and $20,000 is used for qualified expenses while $5,000 is used for spending and travel money, earnings on the $5,000 portion of the distribution are taxable.

In addition, the portion of the distribution representing earnings on contributions is subject to a 10 percent penalty.

Withdrawals from a 529 plan can be made in the same year in which an education credit is claimed, but the same expenses cannot be used for both benefits.

If withdrawals are made from a 529 plan and Coverdell ESA in the same year and the total withdrawal exceeds qualified education expenses, a portion of the withdrawal is taxable. How to figure the taxable portion was explained earlier in the Coverdell Education Savings Accounts section, under "Pitfalls."

Where to Claim the Exclusion

Contributions to qualified tuition programs need not be reported on the return of the contributor or the return of the beneficiary.

Distributions from qualified tuition programs need not be reported if they are tax free. To figure the tax-free portion of distributions, you can use a worksheet for this purpose in IRS Publication 970. For any year in which distributions are made, the 529 plan must send you (and the IRS) an information return, Form 1099-Q, Qualified Tuition Program. For distributions in 2008, the return must be issued no later than January 31, 2009.

Seminars

You've seen the ads: Attend a seminar to learn all about this subject or that. While some seminars are free of charge, others can cost hundreds or even thousands of dollars. From a tax standpoint, the cost of seminars is deductible only under limited circumstances.

Benefit ≋

Job-related seminars may be deducted if the conditions for job-related education discussed earlier in this chapter are met.

No deduction can be claimed for seminars on self-improvement that are not job-related. No deduction can be claimed for investment seminars.

Where on the Return to Claim the Deduction

See job-related education discussed earlier in this chapter.

Educational Travel

Saint Augustine said, "The world is a book, and those who do not travel read only a page." Taxwise, the cost of travel usually is a nondeductible personal expense. But there are exceptions for which the cost of travel may be deductible.

Benefit ≋

They say travel is broadening (a century ago, wealthy young men and women used to "take the grand tour" as a coming-of-age lesson). From a tax perspective, however, a deduction for educational travel is extremely limited. As a general rule, no deduction can be claimed for educational travel. However, this ban does not apply to overseas courses and lectures, the cost of which may qualify for a job-related education deduction.

Conditions

To be deductible as job-related education, travel must meet all of the conditions discussed earlier in this chapter.

Planning Tip

Overseas courses need not be taken for credit to qualify for a deduction. For example, an English teacher who took a course on Greek myths in Greece taught by university professors was allowed a deduction for her travel expenses and course registration fees even though she did not take the courses for credit.

Pitfall

No deduction can be claimed for travel that is merely beneficial. For example, an architect who travels to Europe to view cathedrals there cannot deduct the cost of the trip as an education expense.

Where to Claim the Deduction

See job-related education earlier in this chapter.

Cancellation of a Student Loan

If you are facing mountains of debt from student loans and have opted to get out from under by taking a particular job, you may be able to not only have your loans canceled, but have them canceled without any tax cost to you.

Benefit ⊗

Normally, the cancellation of a loan results in income to the borrower. But under certain conditions, the cancellation of a student loan can be tax free. There is no dollar limit to this benefit.

Example

You take out a government loan to obtain your teaching license. The loan is forgiven if you work for five years as a teacher on a Native American reservation. This debt forgiveness is *not* income to you if you complete the required years of work.

Conditions

You can exclude the debt forgiveness on your student loan from income if you are required to work for a set period of time in a certain profession (e.g., nursing, medicine, or law) for any of a broad class of employers.

The loan must have been made by a qualified lender, which includes:

- The government (federal, state, or local government or an agency of the government)
- A tax-exempt public benefit corporation
- An educational institution if the loan is made under an agreement with the government or a tax-exempt public benefit corporation or under a program designed to encourage students to serve in occupations or areas with unmet needs

Planning Tip

Make sure you fully understand your work obligation in order to secure tax-free treatment for cancellation of your student loan.

Pitfall

If you satisfy only part of the required work and a portion of the loan is forgiven anyway, you must include that portion in income.

Where to Claim the Benefit

If the loan forgiveness is tax free you do not report anything on your return. If cancellation of your student loan is not tax free, you must include the debt forgiveness in income on your return. Report it as "other income." Generally, debt forgiveness that is not tax free is reported to you (and to the IRS) on Form 1099-C, Cancellation of Debt.

Penalty-Free Withdrawals from IRAs

Distributions can be taken from an IRA before age $59^1/_2$ if the funds are used to pay qualified higher education costs for yourself, your spouse, or dependent. The Tax Court has said that funds used to buy a computer are *not* a qualified expense where its use is not required for any course and access to computer-posted course syllabi can be done through school computers in the library.

Withdrawals can be taken penalty-free only in the year in which you pay the expenses.

CHAPTER 4

Your Home

Home ownership is part of the American dream. According to the U.S. Department of Housing and Urban Development, about 70 percent of Americans now own their own homes. There are many reasons that we want to own rather than rent a home—for example, homes have proved to be the one bright spot in our recently poor economy. But there are also sound tax reasons favoring home ownership. Certain expenses of home ownership are deductible. And when you sell your home, some or all of your profit may be tax free. If you had problems with your mortgage or lost your home to foreclosure, there may be special tax breaks for you.

This chapter explains:

- Mortgages
- Mortgage interest tax credit
- Home equity loans
- Points
- Refinancing
- Prepayment penalties
- Late payment penalties
- Mortgage insurance
- Cancellation of mortgage debt
- Penalty-free IRA withdrawals for home-buying expenses
- Homebuyer credit
- Real estate taxes
- Real estate tax rebates for volunteer responders
- Cooperative housing
- Minister's rental allowance
- Home sale exclusion
- Moving expenses
- Energy improvements

Casualties and disasters that can befall your home, and the deductions you can claim for them, are explained in Chapter 13. The home office deduction for using a portion of your home for business is explained in Chapter 5.

For more information, see IRS Publication 521, *Moving Expenses*; IRS Publication 523, *Selling Your Home*; IRS Publication 530, *Tax Information for First-Time Homeowners*; the IRS Publication 936, *Home Mortgage Interest Deduction* and IRS Publication 4681, *Cancelled Debts, Foreclosures, Repossessions, and Abandonments*. See also *J.K. Lasser's Homeowner's Tax Breaks* by Gerald Robinson.

Mortgages

Mortgages are a way to leverage yourself into home ownership: The bank or other lender (called the mortgagee) lends you the funds needed to buy your home over and above your out-of-pocket investment. You become the mortgagor and each month repay a portion of the principal (the money you borrowed), plus interest. While your repayment of principal is *never* deductible, you may be able to deduct your interest payments.

Benefit ⊜

Interest on your home mortgage may be fully deductible as an itemized deduction. There is no dollar limit on the amount of interest you can deduct annually, but there are limits on the size of the mortgage on which the interest is claimed. The mortgage interest rule applies to both fixed and adjustable rate mortgages.

You may deduct interest on so-called "acquisition indebtedness" up to $1 million (or any amount for loans obtained before October 14, 1987). In addition, you can deduct interest on home equity debt up to $100,000 (discussed later in this chapter). Thus, you can deduct interest on total home debt up to $1.1 million. And you can use this rule for your main home plus one additional residence of yours that you designate as your second home.

Conditions

For interest to be fully deductible, you must meet four conditions:

1. Acquisition indebtedness (which is usually a mortgage used to buy or build your home) cannot exceed $1 million. However, this dollar limit does not apply to a mortgage obtained before October 14, 1987.
2. The debt must be secured by the residence.
3. You deduct interest on no more than two residences.
4. You are personally obligated for repayment of the debt.

ACQUISITION INDEBTEDNESS

Acquisition indebtedness is usually a mortgage obtained to buy, build, or substantially improve a home (subject to the two residence limit). If you use the funds to construct your home, only interest paid during the 24-month period starting with the month in which construction begins is deductible. Interest paid before or after this 24-month period is not acquisition indebtedness; it is treated as nondeductible personal interest.

Example

In May 2007, you buy land to build your dream home and obtain a construction loan in June. Construction begins in September 2007, and the home is completed in June 2008. You may deduct interest on the loan starting with interest in September 2007,

the month in which construction began. Since the
home is completed within 24 months, interest
through the end of construction is deductible.

If a loan is taken out within 90 days after construction
is completed, it may still qualify in full as acquisition indebtedness. It qualifies as acquisition indebtedness to the
extent of construction expenses incurred within the last
24 months before the completion of the home, plus expenses
through the date of the loan.

Example

Same as the preceding example, except that in July
2008 you refinance the loan. Since the loan is
obtained within 90 days after building completion, it
qualifies as acquisition indebtedness and interest is
deductible.

How much renovation is required to be considered a substantial improvement to the home? There is no clear rule.
Generally, if you add a room, convert an attic, garage, or base-
ment to living space, or renovate a kitchen, you can safely
treat interest on the loan as acquisition indebtedness. Just
about any type of capital improvement that adds to the basis
of your home constitutes a substantial improvement; a repair
is not a capital improvement, and a loan to make repairs is
not acquisition indebtedness.

A home for this purpose isn't limited to a single-family dwelling. It also includes a condominium or cooperative unit, houseboat, mobile home, or house trailer as long as it has sleeping, cooking, and toilet facilities.

The $1 million limit applies to total acquisition indebtedness; it does not apply on a per-home basis.

DEBT SECURED BY THE HOME

The loan must be secured by your main or second home in order for interest on the loan to be deductible. "Secured" means that the loan is recorded in your city, town, or county recording office or the loan satisfies similar requirements under your state's law that gives the lender the right to foreclose against your home if you fail to repay the loan.

TWO-RESIDENCE LIMIT

A deduction for mortgage interest is limited to two residences: your main home and a second residence. If you have more than two homes, you can select which of the additional homes to designate as your second residence for interest deduction purposes. Obviously, it pays to designate the home with the larger interest payments. You can change your designation from year to year.

If a married couple files jointly, they can designate a second residence as a home even if it is owned or used by one of them. But if they file separately, each spouse generally may deduct interest on debt secured by one home unless they agree in writing to allow one spouse to deduct interest on the main home plus a second residence.

If you rent out a home during the year but use it for personal (nonrental) purposes for more than 14 days or 10 percent of the rental days, you can treat the home as a personal residence for which the interest is deductible. In counting rental days, include any days that the home is held for rental. In counting personal days, include any days your home is used by close family members.

Example

In addition to your main home, you own a beachfront condominium that you rent out through a rental agency two weeks each year at the start of the summer season. You spend the balance of the summer at your unit, so your personal use is sufficient for your home to be treated as a personal residence despite the rental. You can designate your condo as your second residence and deduct interest on the mortgage on the condo.

PERSONAL LIABILITY

To deduct interest on a home mortgage you must be personally obligated for its repayment. If, for example, you are financially unable to obtain a mortgage so your parents help you out by obtaining the loan, you cannot deduct mortgage interest (even if you pay the lender directly rather than repaying your parents). Only they can deduct the interest.

One case did allow a homeowner to deduct interest on a loan obtained by a brother because the homeowner had a poor credit rating, but the facts in the case were unique; the homeowner was contractually obligated to his brother to pay off the mortgage.

Planning Tips

Think hard about the type and amount of mortgage you want to take out when you buy your home. Once you have purchased your home, additional financing generally doesn't qualify as acquisition indebtedness.

When you sell your home, look at the settlement papers to determine the interest charged up to the date of sale so that you don't overlook any interest deduction you may be entitled to claim.

Pitfalls

You cannot deduct your interest if you claim the standard deduction; you must itemize deductions to claim this benefit.

You cannot deduct mortgage fees that you paid to obtain the loan, such as the cost of an appraisal, a credit report, or loan assumption fees. But points paid to obtain the mortgage may be deductible, as discussed later.

You cannot deduct interest on mortgage assistance payments made on your behalf under Section 234 of the National Housing Act.

Where to Claim the Deduction

You deduct home mortgage interest on Schedule A of Form 1040. You cannot claim the deduction if you file Form 1040A or Form 1040EZ. The amount of mortgage interest is reported annually to you by the lender on Form 1098, Mortgage Interest Statement.

Mortgage Interest Tax Credit

The government's policy is to encourage home ownership. To help low-income people become homeowners, the government offers certain assistance, including the opportunity to claim a tax credit for mortgage interest.

Benefit ✚

Even better than deducting your mortgage interest, you may be eligible for a tax credit of up to $2,000 of home mortgage interest paid through mortgage interest certificates. These certificates are issued to certain homeowners as a means of encouraging home ownership. The credit may be claimed regardless of whether you itemize your personal deductions or claim the standard deduction.

If you received a mortgage credit certificate from your state or local government in connection with the purchase or renovation of your main home, you may be entitled to claim a tax credit with respect to your mortgage interest. The amount of the credit is the percentage shown on your mortgage credit certificate multiplied by the lesser of:

- Interest you paid during the year on your actual loan amount
- Interest you paid on the loan amount shown on your mortgage credit certificate

The credit cannot be more than $2,000 if the percentage shown on your mortgage credit certificate is 20 percent or more.

You must reduce your deduction for home mortgage interest by the amount of any credit you claim.

Conditions

You can claim this tax credit only if you meet two conditions:

1. You have received a mortgage credit certificate from your state or local government ("qualified mortgage credit certificate").

2. Your home meets certain requirements ("qualified home").

QUALIFIED MORTGAGE CREDIT CERTIFICATE

You qualify for the credit only if you receive a qualified certificate. Qualified mortgage interest certificates are issued by a state or local government or agency under a qualified mortgage credit certificate program. Certificates issued by the Federal Housing Administration, the Department of Veterans Affairs, and the Farmers Home Administration as well as Homestead Staff Exemption Certificates do not qualify.

QUALIFIED HOME

The home must be your main home. The value of your home cannot exceed a certain value:

- A value of 90 percent of the average area purchase price
- A value of 110 percent of the average area purchase price in certain targeted areas

Planning Tips

If you are thinking about buying a home but do not know if you can afford the payments, you may be able to swing a deal if you qualify for this type of government assistance. For information about special financing programs, visit the

U.S. Department of Housing and Urban Development at www.hud.gov/buying/insured.cfm.

To find out whether you are eligible for a mortgage credit certificate, contact your local housing or redevelopment agency or ask your local real estate agent for information.

If you qualify for the credit and it exceeds your tax liability without regard to other tax credits, you do not lose the credit. Instead, you can carry the excess amount forward to be used in a future year if you are also eligible for the credit in that year.

If you refinance your mortgage, you do not lose your eligibility to claim the credit if your certificate is reissued and the reissued certificate meets five conditions:

1. It must be issued to the original holder of the existing certificate for the same property.

2. It must entirely replace the existing certificate (you cannot retain any portion of the outstanding balance of the existing certificate).

3. The certified indebtedness on the reissued certificate cannot be more than the outstanding balance on the existing certificate.

4. The credit rate of the reissued certificate cannot be more than the credit rate of the existing certificate.

5. The reissued certificate cannot result in a larger amount of interest than is otherwise allowable under the existing certificate for any year.

Pitfalls

You must reduce your deduction for home mortgage interest by the amount of the credit.

If you own your home jointly with a person who is not your spouse, you must divide the credit between the two of you according to your respective ownership interests. If you each own a 50 percent interest in the home, then you are each entitled to one-half of the credit.

If you buy a home using a mortgage credit certificate and sell it within nine years, you may have to repay some of the credit.

Where to Claim the Credit

You figure the credit on Form 8396, Mortgage Interest Certificate, and enter the amount of the credit in the "Tax and Credits" section of Form 1040.

You cannot claim the credit if you file Form 1040A or 1040EZ.

If you are subject to recapture of the credit because you sold your home within nine years of using the mortgage credit certificate, you must complete Form 8828, Recapture of Federal Mortgage Subsidy. You report the recaptured amount in the "Other Payments" section of Form 1040. You must file Form 1040 and cannot file Form 1040A or 1040EZ.

Home Equity Loans

Equity is the amount of money you would receive, over and above any outstanding mortgage, if you were to sell your home today. Equity is built up in two ways: by paying down a mortgage on the home and by appreciation in property values. As your equity increases, you may be able to tap into it *without* selling the home by using a home equity loan. This loan may be the only loan on the property or it may be a second or even third loan in addition to any other home mortgage. The tax law allows interest on home equity loans to be deductible under certain conditions.

Benefit ⊜

You may deduct interest on home equity loans up to $100,000 if you itemize your deductions. There is no dollar limit on the amount of interest you can deduct (the limit applies to the amount of borrowing).

The rules for deducting interest on home equity loans apply to any type of home equity loan: a fixed home equity loan or a home equity line of credit with an adjustable interest rate. The deduction applies regardless of how you spend the proceeds (i.e., you don't have to use them for the home and can spend them in any way you desire, including paying off credit card debt).

Conditions

The same four conditions discussed for mortgage interest earlier (except for a smaller maximum amount) apply to deducting interest on home equity loans in full.

1. Total home equity debt cannot exceed $100,000. In measuring the $100,000 limit, take into account only the amount you've borrowed, not your potential borrowing under a home equity line of credit loan. The $100,000 home equity limit is figured separately from the $1 million home acquisition limit discussed earlier in this chapter, so that interest is deductible on total borrowing up to $1.1 million ($1 million acquisition debt and $100,000 home equity debt).

2. The debt must be secured by the residence.

3. The debt can apply to your main or second home.

4. You are personally obligated for repayment of the debt.

Planning Tips

If the amount of a home equity loan exceeds the $100,000 limit, you treat the interest on the first $100,000 as fully deductible mortgage interest. Interest on the balance of the debt may still be deductible under a tax rule other than home mortgage interest. The treatment of this portion of interest depends on what you use the proceeds for:

- If you use the proceeds to pay personal expenses (e.g., a vacation or credit card debt), it is nondeductible.
- If you use the proceeds to purchase investments (other than tax-exempt securities), you can treat it as investment interest. The rules on deducting investment interest are explained in Chapter 8.
- If you use the proceeds for your business, interest may qualify as fully deductible business interest, as explained in Chapter 5.

Pitfalls

In the case of a reverse mortgage, where a homeowner who is at least age 62 borrows against the equity in the home to pay personal living expenses and does not make mortgage payments (the lender recoups what is owed when the homeowner sells the home or dies), interest is deductible only when the loan is repaid. No deduction can be taken as the interest accrues each month on the outstanding loan.

While interest on home equity debt up to $100,000 is fully deductible for regular tax purposes regardless of what the loan proceeds are used for, such interest is deductible for purposes of the alternative minimum tax only if the proceeds are used to improve your main or second home.

Where to Claim the Deduction

You deduct interest on home equity debt on Schedule A of Form 1040. The amount of mortgage interest is reported annually to you by the lender on Form 1098, Mortgage Interest Statement.

You cannot claim the deduction if you file Form 1040A or Form 1040EZ.

Points

"Points" are additional charges for acquiring a loan. Each point is 1 percent of the loan amount. In general, the more points you pay, the lower your interest rate on the loan. Points generally are deductible; the only question is *when* they can be deducted.

Benefit ⊜

When you take out a mortgage, you may pay points to the lender. Points paid to obtain a home mortgage are deductible as part of your itemized interest deduction. However, points in some cases are deductible in full in the year in which they are paid while in other cases they must be amortized (deducted ratably) over the term of the loan.

Conditions

First determine whether the payment qualifies as "points" (defined next). Then see if the points can be deducted in full in the year of payment or must be deducted over the term of the mortgage.

IMMEDIATE DEDUCTIBILITY

If the loan is taken to buy, build, or substantially improve your main home, you may deduct the points in the year of payment if you meet the following conditions:

- Points are charged for interest and not for services performed by the lender. The designation of the payment, as points, loan origination fees, or otherwise, is not controlling of the tax treatment; it is the purpose for which the money is charged that governs whether you can treat points as interest.

- The loan is secured by your main home. If the loan relates to a second home, you cannot fully deduct the points in the year of payment.

- The charging of points is an established business practice in the geographical area in which you are located.

- The amount of points is computed as a percentage of the loan and specifically earmarked on the loan closing statement as points, loan origination fees, or loan discount.

- You pay the points directly to the lender. Points withheld from the loan proceeds used to buy your main home are treated as having been paid directly to the lender. Points withheld from loan proceeds used to substantially improve your main home are not immediately deductible; you must pay the points with other funds to secure a full deduction in the year of payment. Points paid by the seller are not treated as paid directly to the lender but rather are viewed as an adjustment to the purchase price of the home.

DEDUCTIBLE OVER THE TERM OF THE LOAN

As long as the payments meet the definition of points and are not fees for services performed by the lender but cannot be deducted in full in the year of payment (or you opt not to deduct them in full), they are deducted over the term of the loan.

Example

In 2008, you pay points of $3,600 to obtain a 30-year mortgage for your vacation home. You must amortize the points over 360 months and can deduct $10 per month each year until you've deducted all of the points or pay off the mortgage.

The following are situations in which you amortize the points rather than fully deduct them in the year of payment:

- To buy a second home.
- To substantially improve your main home but the points are withheld from the mortgage.
- To refinance an existing mortgage.
- To buy your main home but you elect to amortize the points.

Planning Tips

If you pay points to buy your main home, you are not required to deduct them in full in the year of payment. You can opt to amortize them over the term of the loan. You may wish to make this election if you can't benefit from the deduction in the year of payment. This might occur if you buy your home late in the year and your total itemized deductions do not exceed your standard deduction amount.

When you are financing a mortgage and faced with the option of paying higher interest with little or no points or a lower interest rate but some or substantial points, which option should you select? The answer usually depends on how long you plan to remain in the home (how long you will be paying the mortgage). To help you make this decision based on your circumstances, use a mortgage points calculator (you can find one at www.dinkytown.net/java/MortgagePoints.html).

Pitfall

If you refinance your loan with a new lender and have been amortizing points over the term of a previous loan (for example, this is your second or third refinance), be sure to deduct the remaining balance of the unamortized points.

Example

In January 2004, when rates had declined below your original mortgage rate, you refinanced your outstanding balance for a new 15-year mortgage, paying $1,800 in points. In July 2008, you refinance

again. On your 2008 return, be sure to deduct the
unamortized points of $1,260: $1,800 ÷ 180
months = $10 per month; 4 years, 6 months × $10 =
$540; $1,800 − $540 = $1,260.

Where to Claim the Deduction

You deduct points along with your home mortgage interest
on Schedule A of Form 1040. There is a separate line on
Schedule A to list your points if they are not included on
Form 1098 with your other home mortgage interest.

You cannot claim the deduction if you file Form 1040A or
Form 1040EZ.

Refinancing

When interest rates decline or a personal credit rating improves, homeowners with existing mortgages can obtain more
favorable terms by refinancing. Generally, this means getting
a new mortgage to replace the old one. But you may borrow
more than you owe on your old loan if the equity in your home
allows for such borrowing—to add a room, pay off credit card
debt, fund a child's education, or take a vacation. Under the
tax law, the treatment of interest depends on what you use
the excess funds for.

Benefit

With interest rates still relatively low, refinancing is a highly
popular strategy to reduce monthly mortgage payments or

obtain additional cash for various purposes. If your home has appreciated in value and/or you have paid down your mortgage, you may be sitting on substantial equity that you can tap by refinancing. You are not taxed on the equity you receive when you refinance your mortgage—the proceeds are tax free.

Example

You bought your home 10 years ago for $100,000, using an $80,000 mortgage, which you've paid down to $72,000. Today your home is worth $225,000. If you refinance for $175,000 and use $72,000 of the proceeds to pay off the old mortgage, you can put $103,000 in your pocket tax free.

Whether and when interest on refinanced debt, as well as points to obtain the new loan, are deductible depend on the purpose of the refinancing (these rules are explained next).

Conditions

Your purpose in refinancing the outstanding debt on your home determines the tax treatment of the interest.

If you refinance your existing acquisition indebtedness, the new loan continues to be treated as acquisition indebtedness so that the interest is fully deductible (assuming the mortgage does not exceed $1 million). It does not matter whether you shorten or lengthen the term of the loan.

If you refinance your existing mortgage to take out equity you've built on in your home, deductibility of the interest on a new mortgage depends on what you do with the proceeds in excess of amounts used to simply refinance the existing debt.

If you use the excess proceeds to pay off credit card debt or other personal expenses, this portion of the debt is treated as home equity debt subject to the $100,000 limit. If the excess debt used for personal purposes exceeds this amount, a portion of your interest is nondeductible.

Example

Your home today is worth $500,000 and the remaining balance of your old mortgage is $200,000. If you refinance for $350,000 and use $50,000 of the proceeds to buy a personal car, take a vacation, and pay off some credit card debt, you can deduct interest on only $300,000 ($200,000 of acquisition indebtedness and $100,000 of home equity debt).

If you use the excess proceeds to substantially improve your home, such as remodel the kitchen or add a family room, interest on this portion of the debt, as well as the portion used to pay off the existing mortgage, is treated as acquisition indebtedness, which is fully deductible if the total does not exceed $1 million.

Example

Same as the preceding example except you use the $50,000 to add a family room to your home. Now you can deduct all of the interest on the new loan ($250,000 of acquisition indebtedness and $100,000 of home equity debt).

Planning Tip

If this is a subsequent refinancing (you've already refinanced your original acquisition indebtedness at least once), points paid on the prior refinancing become fully deductible in the year of your latest refinancing.

Example

In January 2004, you refinanced your original mortgage and paid $3,600 for a 30-year loan. In January 2008, when interest rates have again declined, you refinance the outstanding balance of the 2004 loan. Of the points paid in 2004, you have already deducted $480 ($120 for 2004, 2005, 2006, and 2007). On your 2008 return you can deduct $3,120, the remaining amount of points on your 2004 refinancing.

Pitfall

If you refinance, consider what term you want for the new loan. If, for example, you have been paying off a 30-year mortgage and have only 22 years remaining, when you refinance do you want to start the clock over again with a new 30-year mortgage? Maybe the answer is yes just to keep monthly payments as low as possible. But you may opt for a shorter term, such as 15, 20, or 25 years, so that you will pay off the mortgage at or about the same time as you had originally planned.

Where to Claim the Benefits

Since the equity you receive on refinancing for more than your old mortgage is not taxable income, you do not have to report it on your return.

You deduct home mortgage interest (including home equity debt and points) on Schedule A of Form 1040. The amount of mortgage interest is reported annually to you by the lender on Form 1098, Mortgage Interest Statement.

You cannot claim the deduction if you file Form 1040A or Form 1040EZ.

Prepayment Penalties

It costs a lender money to make a loan, which it expects to recoup through interest collected during the term of the loan. But if a borrower pays off a loan within a short time of obtaining it (generally under two years), the lender has not had time to recoup its lending costs. To protect the lender against a quick payoff, prepayment penalties may be owed. The prepayment penalties are spelled out in the mortgage note at the time of obtaining the mortgage. From the borrower's perspective, the tax law looks favorably on prepayment penalties, allowing them to be deductible if certain conditions are met.

Benefit ⊜

If you pay off your mortgage or home equity debt before you are required to, there may be a prepayment penalty as specified in your mortgage papers. Prepayment penalties are treated as deductible interest—they are a set amount of interest—for example, six months of interest on 80 percent of your outstanding loan balance) if you pay off the mortgage before a set term (usually one to two years). For the rules on deducting interest on your home or second home, see earlier in this chapter.

Conditions

There are no special conditions to meet for deducting prepayment penalties. Simply refer to the rules discussed earlier in this chapter on how to treat mortgage interest.

Planning Tip

Think ahead. When taking out a mortgage, check whether there are any potential prepayment penalties. You may be able to get the lender to delete these from the loan agreement. This is important because you may have to relocate before you had planned and do not want to incur this needless cost.

Pitfall

Don't sign any mortgage loan agreement before finding out if there are prepayment penalties. One common scam by unscrupulous lenders is nondisclosure of prepayment penalties, which can run as much as six months of interest on up to 80 percent of the outstanding loan balance. Such a high penalty can keep you locked into a mortgage when you otherwise could have refinanced for a lower mortgage rate.

Where to Claim the Deduction on Your Return

Assuming that the prepayment payment penalty is deductible, you claim it with your home mortgage interest on Schedule A of Form 1040. The amount of mortgage interest is reported annually to you by the lender on Form 1098, Mortgage Interest Statement.

You cannot claim the deduction if you file Form 1040A or Form 1040EZ.

Late Payment Penalties

Under the terms of a loan, if a payment is late for any reason the borrower may owe additional amounts called late payment penalties. There are different types of late payment penalties: a flat fee, such as $25, charged without regard to the amount of the late payment or how long it is outstanding, and a percentage fee, fixed with regard to the late payment. The percentage fee continues to be accessed each month that a payment remains delinquent. Only late payment penalties qualifying as "interest" may be deductible.

Benefit ⊜

If you are late in making a payment, you may be charged a penalty by the lender. Generally, penalties for delinquent payments are treated as deductible interest, which can be written off if you itemize your deductions.

Example

Your monthly mortgage payment is $1,000, which is subject to a 2 percent late payment penalty. Due to unexpected financial reverses, you fail to make your payment for June, July, and August. In September, you're back on your feet and pay up all outstanding amounts, including the late payment penalties of $120 (June payment: 2% of $1,000 × 3 months; July payment: 2% of $1,000 × 2 months; August payment: 2% of $1,000 × 1 month). Since the late payment penalties are an interest charge, they are deductible.

Condition

Late payment penalties are treated as deductible interest as long as they are not imposed for a specific service provided by the lender. If they are a flat charge imposed regardless of how late the delinquency may be, they are viewed as a nondeductible service charge rather than as deductible interest.

Planning Tip

Even though late payment penalties can be deductible, you should try to avoid them if possible. The deduction does not fully offset your payment. One way to do so is to arrange for mortgage payments to be debited automatically from your checking account.

Pitfall

Being late on making your mortgage payments can cost you more than late payment penalties. Being late can adversely affect your credit rating and hurt your ability to obtain a loan or even get a job within two years or so of the late payment. Usually if your payment is no more than 30 days late, it will not show up on your credit report. But anything later will be reported by the lender to the major credit reporting bureaus and can affect your creditworthiness for about two years.

Where to Claim the Deduction on Your Return

Assuming that the late payment penalty is deductible, you claim it with your home mortgage interest on Schedule A of Form 1040. The amount of mortgage interest is reported annually to you by the lender on Form 1098, Mortgage Interest Statement.

You cannot claim the deduction if you file Form 1040A or Form 1040EZ.

Mortgage Insurance

If you put less than 20 percent down to purchase your home, you may be required to carry private mortgage insurance (PMI) on the shortfall to protect the lender from a default.

The cost of PMI typically runs from 0.6 percent to 0.8 percent of the loan amount. Payments of mortgage insurance obtained in 2008 may result in a tax deduction.

Benefit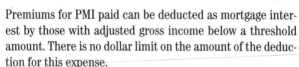

Premiums for PMI paid can be deducted as mortgage interest by those with adjusted gross income below a threshold amount. There is no dollar limit on the amount of the deduction for this expense.

Conditions

To qualify for this itemized deduction, two conditions must be met:

- The insurance must be first obtained in 2007, 2008, 2009, or 2010. This insurance is available through commercial insurers as well as through federal loan programs such as the Veterans Administration (VA), the Rural Housing Administration (RHA), and the Federal Housing Administration (FHA).

- To claim the full deduction, your adjusted gross income cannot exceed $100,000 ($50,000 for married persons filing separate returns). Any deduction is reduced by one dollar for each dollar in excess of the AGI limit; no deduction is allowed if AGI exceeds $110,000 ($60,000 for married persons filing separate returns).

Planning Tip

PMI may be a way to help you buy a home even though you haven't yet saved the full down payment.

Once the equity in your home, from making payments on your mortgage as well as appreciation in property value, reaches 20 percent, cancel the mortgage insurance.

Pitfall

There is no downside to claiming this deduction. However, it applies only through 2009 unless Congress extends the law.

Where to Claim the Deduction

The deduction is reported on Schedule A of Form 1040. You cannot claim the deduction if you file Form 1040A or Form 1040EZ.

Cancellation of Mortgage Debt

During the subprime mortgage debacle, thousands of Americans have lost their homes. Homeowners are usually personally liable for the amount of the mortgage, even though the lender can foreclose, sell the home, and use the sale proceeds to pay down the debt. Unfortunately, in today's real estate market, the borrower may still owe money on the loan after foreclosure (the home sale may not cover what's due). Generally, when the lender forgives a portion of the outstanding mortgage, a practice that lets the borrower off the hook, this debt forgiveness is considered to be ordinary income for tax purposes. Under the Mortgage Forgiveness Debt Relief Act of 2007, forgiven debt on a main home in 2007–2012 may not be taxable.

Benefit ⊜

The debt forgiveness is treated as tax-free income, regardless of the amount of the debt that's forgiven (within the limit below).

Conditions

There are two conditions for tax-free treatment:

- The forgiven debt must have been used to buy, build, or substantially improve your main home and the debt must have been secured by the home. If a debt has been refinanced, the amount qualifying for this tax break is limited to the mortgage principal immediately before the refinancing.
- The limit on qualifying debt is $2 million ($1 million for a married person filing separately).

Planning Tip

Debt forgiveness can apply to a so-called short sale, which occurs when the amount of the outstanding debt is greater than value of the home (what a lender would realize if the home were sold). The short sale avoids the need for fore-closure. Also, some lenders will work with a homeowner to reduce the mortgage balance or change the terms of the loan so the homeowner can stay in his or her home. If there is any cancellation of debt, it can be tax free to the same extent as cancellation related to a foreclosure.

Pitfalls

The tax break on forgiven debt does not apply to a second home, rental property, or business property. You may still have to recognize gain if the home was foreclosed upon and the amount realized on the sale is greater than your basis in the home. The fair market value of the property (reported to the borrower in Box 7 of Form 1099-C, Cancellation of Debt) is treated as the amount realized on the sale. If you sell your home at a loss, you cannot deduct the loss; it is a nondeductible personal loss.

Where to Claim the Benefit

Forgiven debt is reported to you by the lender on Form 1099-C. To claim the exclusion, complete Form 982, Reduction of Tax Attributes Due to Discharge of Indebtedness (instructions to the form point out the specific lines applicable to home mortgage debt forgiveness). There is no income from debt cancellation to report on the return; just attach the completed Form 982 to the return.

Penalty-Free IRA Withdrawals for Home-Buying Expenses

If you thought IRAs were for retirement only, you'd be wrong. The tax law lets you tap into your IRA for certain special reasons without incurring any penalty (although withdrawals are subject to tax). One of those reasons is to buy a home.

Benefit ⊗

You may be able to use money in your IRA toward the cost of buying a home without incurring an early distribution penalty from your IRA. The withdrawal is subject to regular income tax, but you avoid the 10 percent early distribution penalty on withdrawals before age $59\frac{1}{2}$.

Condition

You can only withdraw up to $10,000 free from penalty from your IRA. This is a once-in-a-lifetime opportunity. If you have already used this break to buy a previous home, you can't use it again.

You must spend the $10,000 on qualified first-time home-buying expenses, such as a down payment to purchase a home. These are expenses used to buy, build, or rehabilitate a main home for yourself, your spouse, child, grandchild, or ancestor (parent or grandparent) of you or your spouse. Such person cannot have had an ownership interest in a principal residence within two years before the purchase, construction, or renovation of the new home.

Planning Tip

Use this tax break only as a last resort. Once you withdraw the funds from the IRA and spend them on home-buying expenses, you cannot replace the funds in your retirement savings account. In effect, you lose the opportunity to build up your retirement savings.

Pitfall

If you take a withdrawal from your IRA with the intention of using the money to buy a home but the sale falls through, you become taxed on the money unless you redeposit it back in the IRA. You have 120 days from your initial withdrawal to take this action.

When a couple is buying a home together, each must be a first-time homebuyer for the penalty exception to apply.

Where to Claim the Benefit

If you take money from your IRA, you must file Form 5329, Additional Taxes on Qualified Plans (Including IRAs) and Other Tax-Favored Accounts. You report total early distributions from your IRA. You can then subtract those exempt from the 10 percent penalty because you used them for qualified first-time home-buying expenses. You must indicate on the appropriate line on the form which exception to the 10 percent penalty you are relying on (a number is assigned to each exception, and these numbers are listed in the instructions to this form).

Since you do not have any penalty on the distribution, you do not report anything in the section of Form 1040 for "Additional Taxes."

If you take money out of your IRA, you *must* file Form 1040 even if you are not subject to a penalty; you cannot file Form 1040A or 1040EZ.

Homebuyer Credit

The federal government wants to encourage home ownership. Toward this end, from time to time, it has provided a tax credit to new buyers. At the time this book went to press, there are two tax credits: (1) a credit for first-time homebuyers in the District of Columbia and (2) a new refundable tax credit for first-time homebuyers anywhere that would be capped at $7,500 ($3,750 for married persons filing separately) and must repaid in most cases.

Benefit ⊕

For the D.C. homebuyer credit, you can claim a tax credit of up to $5,000 ($2,500 if married filing separately) for the purpose of buying a home in the District of Columbia if certain conditions are met. For the first-time homebuyer credit, you can claim a refundable credit of 10 percent of the purchase price for a home bought after April 9, 2008, and before July 1, 2009, but no more than $7,500 ($3,750 for married filing separately). This credit is merely an interest-free loan from the government (see below).

Conditions

To claim the credit you must meet two conditions:

1. You must be a first-time homebuyer in D.C. for the D.C. credit or anywhere else for the other credit.
2. Your modified adjusted gross income cannot exceed set limits.

FIRST-TIME HOMEBUYER

Being a first-time homebuyer doesn't mean you've *never* owned a home. To qualify as a first-time homebuyer for the D.C. credit, you (and your spouse) must not have owned a home in the District of Columbia within one year preceding the date of the purchase of your D.C. home (three years preceding the date of purchase for the first-time homebuyer credit).

The credit applies only to the purchase of your main home; you cannot use the credit for the purchase of a second home.

MAGI LIMIT

The amount of the credit you can claim, if any, depends on your modified adjusted gross income (MAGI). MAGI for this purpose is adjusted gross income increased by the foreign earned income exclusion and certain other foreign items.

You can claim a full credit only if your modified adjusted gross income is below the phaseout range found in Table 4.1. You can claim a partial credit if your MAGI is within the phaseout range; no credit may be claimed if your MAGI exceeds the phaseout range.

Planning Tip

If the amount of credit exceeds your tax liability (reduced by certain other credits), you don't lose the credit. Instead, you can carry over the unused credit to succeeding tax years.

Pitfall

The credit is a one-time credit, so if you claimed this credit before, you cannot use it again, even if you meet eligibility conditions.

TABLE 4.1 Phaseout Ranges for the Homebuyer Credit[5]

Filing Status*	D.C. Credit MAGI	First-Time Homebuyer Credit MAGI
Joint return	$110,000–130,000	$150,000–170,000
Unmarried	$ 70,000–90,000	$ 75,000–95,000

*You cannot claim the credit if you are married filing separately.

Example

You bought a D.C. home in December 2000 and sold it in 2003. You rented a home until you bought a new main home in the District of Columbia in May 2008. Since you claimed the credit on your 2000 return, you cannot claim the credit again for your purchase in 2008, even though you otherwise meet the conditions of a first-time homebuyer.

The first-time homebuyer credit must be repaid in equal installments over 15 years beginning in the second year after claiming the credit. For instance, if a $7,500 credit is claimed for a home purchased in September 2008, $500 must be reported as income starting with the 2010 return. Accelerated recapture is required if the home is sold or ceases to be used as a principal residence before the end of the 15-year recapture period. No recapture is required, however, if the homeowner dies, or transfers the home to a spouse incident to divorce (that spouse becomes responsible for recapture. Special rules apply for involuntary conversions.

Where to Claim the Credit

You figure the D.C. credit on Form 8859, District of Columbia First-Time Homebuyer Credit, and enter the credit amount in the "Tax and Credits" section of Form 1040. The first-time homebuyer credit is figured on Form 5405, First-time Homebuyers Credits, and entered in the "Payments" section of Form 1040.

You cannot claim this credit if you file Form 1040A or 1040EZ.

Real Estate Taxes

Property owners are charged real estate taxes to cover government services related to the property. Local property taxes may include city, town, and/or county taxes; school taxes; and even other charges (such as fire or sewer district taxes). Fortunately, the tax law allows property owners to deduct these taxes.

Benefit ⊜

Your burden of paying local property taxes, including city, town, and/or county taxes and school taxes, can be eased somewhat by deducting your payments.

If you itemize deductions, you can deduct real estate taxes you pay on your main home and any other home you own. There are no limits on the dollar amount of real estate taxes you can deduct. There are no limits on the number of homes for which you can claim the deduction. The deduction for real estate taxes on your residence and vacation homes is claimed as an itemized deduction (you cannot use this benefit if you claim the standard deduction). If you claim the standard deduction, you can deduct $500 ($1000 on a joint return) for property taxes on your principal residence in 2008 and 2009 (see Chapter One).

If you pay real estate taxes on a rental property, it is deductible against your rental income, regardless of whether you itemize your personal deductions.

Conditions

You must be the owner of the home so that you are obligated for the payment of the tax. If you buy the property at a tax sale, you cannot start to deduct property taxes until you receive title to the property under state law (typically following a redemption period).

If you pay the seller's unpaid back taxes when you purchase the home, you cannot deduct this payment as your taxes. You can add the payment to your basis in the home used for figuring gain or loss when you sell it.

In the year that property is sold, real estate taxes must be allocated between the buyer and the seller. (Generally this allocation is reflected in your closing papers.)

- The seller can deduct taxes for the portion of the year through the day before the date of sale.
- The buyer can deduct taxes for the portion of the year commencing with the date of sale.

Generally if you rent rather than own your home, you cannot deduct the portion of the rent that the landlord uses to pay the property taxes. However, in Hawaii you can do so if the lease runs for 15 years or more. Also, as a tenant in California you can deduct your payments if you have your name placed on the tax rolls and agree to pay the tax directly to the taxing authority.

Planning Tips

Consider prepaying an upcoming tax bill before the end of the year to increase your current deductions. For example, pay your January 2009 property tax bill in December 2008 to increase your deductions for 2008.

Ask your city or town whether you qualify for any property tax reductions or rebates. Some areas provide them on the basis of age (reduction for seniors), veteran status, or for some other reason. Some locations even suspend real estate taxes for seniors entirely until the home is sold (e.g., when the owner dies or relocates). Generally, a reduction or rebate is not automatic; the homeowner must apply for it. The amount saved because of a property tax reduction or rebate is *not* treated as income; it merely lowers the amount you pay for real estate taxes and, in turn, the amount of your itemized deduction for real estate taxes.

Pitfalls

If you make payments to the lender that are held in escrow and disbursed to the taxing authority, you can only deduct real estate taxes when the lender makes the disbursements (not when you pay the lender).

If title to your home is in the name of one spouse and the other spouse pays the real estate tax bill, the deduction can be claimed only if you file a joint return. Since the party paying the tax isn't the legal owner of the home, the tax may not be deducted on a separate return.

Special assessments by homeowners associations for the purpose of maintaining common areas or special assessments by municipalities for certain government services (water, sewage, or garbage collection) are not deductible as real estate taxes.

Do not prepay real estate taxes if you are subject to the alternative minimum tax. Since taxes are not deductible for AMT purposes, prepaying them can trigger or increase your

AMT liability. Effectively you lose the benefit of claiming the deduction.

If you receive a homestead tax credit from your state based on a percentage of your real estate taxes, the IRS says that the credit is treated for federal tax purposes as a reduction in your state income tax. This limits the amount of state income tax you can claim as an itemized deduction on your federal income tax return; it doesn't change your deduction for real property taxes.

Where to Claim the Deduction

You deduct your payment of real estate taxes on your residence and vacation homes as an itemized deduction on Schedule A of Form 1040 (or as an additional standard deduction within limits if you don't itemize). You deduct real estate taxes on rental properties on Schedule E of Form 1040.

You cannot deduct property taxes on a personal residence or rental property if you file Form 1040A or 1040EZ.

In the year you sell property, if your share of real estate taxes is paid in advance by the buyer, the lender or real estate broker will generally include this information on Form 1099-S, Proceeds from Real Estate Transactions. But this form is not required to be filed for all sales, so you should keep track of this information (check your settlement papers).

Each year that you own property you do *not* receive any official information return notifying you of the amount of taxes you paid during the year. As a practical matter, if you make payments to a commercial lender to cover real estate taxes, your annual tax payments will be detailed in a year-end statement sent to you by the lender.

Real Estate Tax Rebate for Volunteer Responders

According to the National Volunteer Fire Council, in 2007 there were about 30,000 fire and emergency medical service (EMS) agencies nationwide, with more than 800,000 volunteer firefighters alone. Under the Mortgage Forgiveness Debt Relief Act of 2007, volunteer firefighters and emergency medical responders can claim some tax relief for their unpaid efforts in the form of an income exclusion.

Benefit ✚

Volunteer emergency responders who receive a state or local tax benefit can exclude up to $360 per year. The benefit can come in the form of a tax reduction or a tax rebate. In most locations, the break is tied to home ownership in the form of a property tax reduction or rebate.

This break applies only for 2008, 2009, and 2010 unless Congress extends it.

Conditions

The break applies only to members of a qualified volunteer emergency response organization. This is an organization created to provide firefighting or emergency medical services for those within the state or locality.

The maximum exclusion is $30 per month multiplied by the number of months in which the person provides services. Someone who is an active volunteer firefighter for the entire year, for example, can exclude $360 ($30 × 12).

Planning Tip

To obtain a tax reduction or rebate, the volunteer usually must apply for it; the government does not ordinarily give this break automatically, so check what paperwork needs to be completed if you qualify. If your taxes are escrowed throughout the year, inform the party holding the escrow account (typically your mortgage lender) to reduce your monthly escrow payments accordingly. There is no downside to claiming this tax break.

Pitfall

Those who qualify to exclude the tax reduction or rebate cannot claim a double deduction by also deducting the tax; no double deduction is allowed.

Where to Claim the Benefit

You do not have to report the tax reduction or rebate; it is tax-free income to you.

Cooperative Housing

Cooperative housing, also called a co-op, is a form of home ownership. You become a tenant-stockholder in a cooperative housing corporation (CHC) that owns and runs a multiunit housing complex. Your shares entitle you to exclusive use of your housing unit, plus access to common areas. There are tax breaks unique to this form of home ownership.

Benefits 🖁

You may experience two levels of deductions—one that is allocated to you from the CHC and the other that you obtain through your direct payments. For example, you may incur two interest deductions—one for your share of interest on debt of the CHC (e.g., for common areas) and one for the purchase of your unit that you financed through a bank. This section discusses only your allocated deduction; deductions for your direct payments are included in other sections of this chapter (e.g., home mortgage interest).

Condition

The only condition for claiming a deduction for CHC expenses allocated to you is ownership of shares in the CHC.

Planning Tip

Tenant-stockholders in cooperative housing corporations are treated the same in the tax law as homeowners of condominiums and single-family homes.

Pitfall

While a tenant-shareholder of an apartment in a cooperative housing corporation can deduct his/her share of the co-op's real estate taxes, a federal appeals court has decided that these taxes are *not* deductible for purposes of the alternative minimum tax (AMT). Even though the AMT rules do not specifically bar a deduction, these taxes are treated in the same manner as if the taxes had been paid directly by the owner of a single-family home.

Where to Claim the Deduction

You claim a deduction for your share of the CHC's mortgage interest and real estate taxes allocated to you on Schedule A of Form 1040 as a "Miscellaneous Itemized Deduction." This deduction is not subject to the 2 percent of AGI limitation.

You cannot deduct your allocated mortgage interest and real estate taxes if you file Form 1040A or 1040EZ.

The CHC should provide you with Form 1098, Mortgage Interest Statement, to show your share of these expenses.

Home Sale Exclusion

Homeowners are highly favored under the tax law. Not only can they deduct certain costs of home ownership, such as mortgage interest and property taxes, but they can also receive tax-free income when they sell their homes. A special rule permits a limited amount of gain from the sale of a main home to escape federal income tax. And this tax break can be used over and over again.

Benefit ⊗

If you sell your home for a profit, you may avoid tax on some or all of your gain as long as you meet certain conditions. More specifically, you do not pay any tax on gain up to $250,000 from the sale of your home ($500,000 on a joint return or by a surviving spouse if the sale is within two years of the other spouse's death) if you owned and used the home as your main residence for at least two of the five years preceding the date of sale. The amount you exclude is tax-free income to you.

Conditions

To be eligible to use the full exclusion amount of $250,000 ($500,000 on a joint return or for a surviving spouse), you must meet all three conditions:

1. The home must be your main home ("principal residence").

2. You owned your home for at least two years prior to the sale.

3. You used your home as your main home for at least two years prior to the sale.

If you acquired your home in a tax-free exchange, the ownership and use periods must be five full years (instead of two of five years) before qualifying for the exclusion.

If you are a member of the uniformed services, Foreign Service, or intelligence community, or are a Peace Corps volunteer, you can elect to suspend the five-year testing period for the ownership and use tests for up to 10 years.

MAIN HOME

Your main home is the one in which you primarily dwell. If you own two or more homes, you must determine which one is your primary residence. This determination is usually based on which one you live in for the greater part of the year. However, this isn't a bright line test; you can use other factors to show that the home you used less of the time is your main home. Such factors include:

- Where you work or own a business
- Where your family members reside
- The address you use for your federal and state income tax returns
- The address you use for your bills and correspondence
- Where you have your driver's license and voter registration
- The location of religious institutions and clubs you belong to

Your main home isn't limited to a single-family dwelling. You can treat as your main home a mobile home, trailer, houseboat, or condominium apartment used as your primary residence. Even stock in a cooperative housing corporation is subject to this rule as long as you live in the cooperative apartment or house as your main home.

If you change the title to your home, you don't necessarily lose the opportunity to claim the exclusion.

- If you transfer ownership of your home to a grantor trust, one in which you are treated as the owner of the trust and report all of the trust's income on your personal tax return, the trust can use the exclusion provided you meet the ownership and use tests.

- If you transfer ownership of your home to a one-member limited liability company, again, the LLC can use the exclusion provided you meet the ownership and use tests. The LLC is treated as a "disregarded entity" for tax purposes so you report all of the LLC's income on your personal tax return.

- If you divorce and title to the home is changed from your spouse's name or joint name to your name alone, you can include the period of your spouse's ownership in meeting the ownership test.

- If you are a surviving spouse, you can use the $500,000 exclusion amount if you sell the home in the year of your spouse's death. But if you sell in a later year, you are limited to the $250,000 exclusion.

OWNERSHIP TEST

You must own your home for at least two years in the aggregate prior to the date of sale. This means that you owned the home for a full 24 months or 730 days (365×2) during the five-year period that ends on the date of sale. The periods of ownership and use need not be continuous or identical.

If you are married and file a joint return, only one spouse is required to meet the ownership test to qualify for the exclusion as long as both satisfy the use test.

USE TEST

You must use your home as your primary residence for at least two years in the aggregate prior to the date of sale. This means that you lived in the home for a full 24 months or 730 days (365×2) during the five-year period that ends on the date of sale. The periods of ownership and use need not be continuous or identical.

Example

In November 2005, you purchased your home and lived there until September 2006 when you took a one-year sabbatical overseas. You returned to your home in September 2007 and lived there until you sold the home in December 2008. You meet the ownership test because you lived in your home for 26 months (10 months before the sabbatical and 16 months after it).

Temporary absences (for example, a three-week vacation) are ignored. This is true even if you rent out your home while you are away.

If a homeowner becomes incapacitated before meeting the two-year use test and resides in a licensed care facility, the full home sale exclusion can be used as long as the home-owner used the home for at least one year prior to moving from the home and meets the two-year ownership test.

PARTIAL EXCLUSION

Even if you sell before meeting the full two-year ownership and use tests, you may be eligible to use a prorated exclusion amount for the period of your ownership and use. A partial exclusion is allowed if you sell early because of:

- *Change in jobs.* If you relocate for a new job or a new business (if self-employed), you automatically are treated as having a qualified change in jobs if the distance test used for the moving expense deduction (explained later in this chapter) is met. The distance between your new job location and your former home must be at least 50 miles greater than the distance between your old job location and your former home. If your spouse, co-owner, or person who resides with you has a change of jobs, you can qualify for the exclusion.

- *Health reasons.* The change must be medically moti-vated (for example, your doctor recommends a change so you can receive medical or personal care for an ill-ness or injury. A change that is merely beneficial to your health (for example, moving to a warmer climate) isn't viewed as a health reason for purposes of using the partial exclusion. Again, the health of your spouse, co-owner, or person who resides with you can be taken into account in determining your eligibility for the partial exclusion.

- *Unforeseen circumstances.* If you are forced to sell be-cause of events beyond your control, you can use the partial exclusion. Such events include, but are not limited to: Your home is destroyed through acts of war or terrorism, someone in your household dies or goes on unemployment benefits, you become unable to pay basic living expenses because of a change in employment (e.g., being furloughed for six months) or self-employment, there is a legal divorce or separation, you have multiple births resulting from the same pregnancy, you must have a larger home to meet adoption agency requirements, you received death threats at the current address, you must leave a senior retirement home so your young grandchild can live with you, you must move to a home that can accommodate your paralyzed mother's disability, you are forced to sell because of pressure from neighbors, you experience excessive airport noise that was not disclosed by the seller, or you become part of a blended family that cannot be accommodated in your current home.

Planning Tips

If you have owned your home for a long time and paid down the mortgage, your gain may exceed your exclusion amount. You can minimize your gain by adding to the basis of your home any capital improvements you've made to it.

EXAMPLES OF CAPITAL IMPROVEMENTS

Addition of a deck, garage, porch, or room

Appliances

Duct work

Fencing

Heating and cooling systems

Kitchen and bathroom modernization

New roof

Paving the driveway

Satellite dish

Security system

Storm doors and windows

Wiring upgrade

If you subdivide your property, selling off vacant land separately from the parcel on which the home is situated, you can claim the exclusion for the sale of the vacant land and the sale of the home provided they occur within two years of each other. However, only one exclusion amount applies to both sales.

Example

You are single in 2008 and subdivide your property and sell the vacant land for a profit of $100,000 (you must allocate the basis in your home between the vacant land and the parcel with the home to determine your gain on the sale of each parcel). You can exclude this gain on your 2008 return. In 2009, you sell the parcel containing your home for a profit of $200,000. You can exclude $150,000 of this $200,000 gain on your 2009 return (you already used $100,000 of the exclusion on your 2008 return). You must report and pay tax on the remaining $50,000 profit.

If you have been claiming a home office deduction for a portion of the home, you can still apply the exclusion to the home office portion as long as both the personal and business portions are part of the same dwelling.

You can use the exclusion over and over again. As long as you meet the two-year ownership and use tests for each residence, you can avoid tax on gains from each one. One exclusion can be claimed every two years.

You aren't required to use the exclusion. You may wish to waive it by reporting your gain if you expect to sell another home shortly at a more substantial profit and wish that home to qualify for the exclusion.

Example

You own two homes, a house in New Jersey and a condominium in Arizona. You've owned each home for many years. In 2008, you sell your New Jersey home to relocate full-time to Arizona. You can use the exclusion for gain from the sale of the New Jersey home in 2008. In 2009, you build a house in Arizona and place your condominium on the market. You sell it in 2010 and can use the exclusion for any gain from the sale of your condominium.

If your home is destroyed by a casualty and insurance proceeds exceed the basis of your home, resulting in a taxable gain, the transaction may qualify as a home sale for purposes of the home sale exclusion. The damage to the home must be sufficient to constitute a "destruction."

Pitfalls

If you have been claiming a home office deduction for a portion of your home, you must recapture depreciation you have claimed for the office after May 6, 1997. This is so even though you can use the exclusion for gain on this part of the home. "Recapture" means you pay tax on all the depreciation claimed after May 6, 1997, at the rate of 25 percent (assuming your tax bracket is at or above this rate). Home office deduction rules are discussed in Chapter 5.

You must reduce the basis of your home by the amount of any energy credit claimed. For example, if you claimed a $200 tax credit in 2007 for installing new storm doors, you must subtract $200 from the basis of your home.

If you fail the two-year ownership and use test, you cannot claim a partial home sale exclusion based on unforeseen circumstances merely because a job promotion, house appreciation, or winning the lottery enables you to buy a bigger home.

Where to Claim the Exclusion

If your gain is fully excludable, you do not have to report the sale of your home on your return. If, however, some of the gain is taxable because it exceeds the exclusion amount (or all of your gain is taxable because you opt *not* to use the exclusion), you report the sale on Schedule D of Form 1040.

You can use a worksheet in IRS Publication 523 to figure your gain and whether any portion of the gain is excludable.

Moving Expenses

According to the U.S. Census Bureau, 42 million Americans move each year (about 14 percent of the population);

individuals will move 11.7 times during their lives. The cost of a move may be high—$10,000 and up in some cases. From a tax perspective, deductibility of moving costs depends on the reason for the move and satisfying certain conditions.

Benefit ① ⊗

When you sell your home and move your things to a new residence because of a change in your work location, you may be able to deduct moving expenses as an adjustment to gross income, even if you don't itemize your other deductions. There is no dollar limit on this benefit.

Deductible amounts include amounts paid to pack, crate, and move your household goods and personal effects. Storage and insurance costs can be treated as deductible expenses for any period within 30 days after the items were moved from your old home but before they were delivered to your new home. If you move overseas, there is no limit on storage and insurance costs while you work at your overseas location. The cost of connecting or disconnecting household appliances is a deductible moving expense, but the cost of installing a telephone in your new home is not deductible.

Deductible amounts also include travel expenses for you and members of your household.

EXAMPLES OF DEDUCTIBLE TRAVEL EXPENSES FOR THE MOVING DEDUCTION

- Lodging en route from the old home to the new home. Include the cost of lodging before you depart for one day after your old residence is unusable as well as lodging for the day of arrival at your new location before you move into your home. However, the cost of meals is not deductible.

- Transportation from the old home to the new home. You and members of your household do not have to travel together; simply add up the costs for each person.

- Your car expenses at 19 cents per mile for the first half of 2008 and 27 cents per mile for the second half of 2008, or your actual out-of-pocket costs for oil, gas, and repairs, if any, for the move. You can also deduct parking and tolls, regardless of which deduction method you use.

If your employer pays to relocate you, reimbursements or employer payments on your behalf are not income if you would have been able to deduct the expenses had you paid for them yourself (i.e., you meet the deduction conditions given next). Such reimbursement need not be included on your Form W-2 if the benefit is excludable. Of course, reimbursements for nondeductible expenses, such as premove house-hunting expenses, are reported on your W-2 and taxable to you as income.

Conditions

To be treated as a deductible expense (or to qualify as a tax-free fringe benefit if paid by the employer), the expense must meet two tests:

1. A distance test
2. A time test

DISTANCE TEST

The distance from your new workplace must be at least 50 miles farther from your old home than your old workplace was. If you relocate to a distant city or across the country, there's no question that you satisfy the distance test. But if you relocate within the same general area, make sure that the move meets the distance test.

Example

Your old workplace was five miles from your old home. Your new workplace is 75 miles from your old home. Since the difference is more than 50 miles, you meet the distance test.

If you are a member of the armed forces, you do not have to meet the distance test if the move is due to a permanent change of station. A permanent change of station includes a move in connection with retirement or termination of active duty if it is within one year of such retirement or termination.

TIME TEST

If you are an employee, you must work full-time in the area of your new workplace for at least 39 weeks during the 12-month period following your move. If you change from being self-employed to being an employee, you must meet the 39-week test as an employee and cannot use any weeks of self-employment for this purpose.

If you are self-employed, you must work full-time in the area of your new workplace for 78 weeks during the 24-month period following your move. If you change from being an employee to being self-employed, you can include any weeks of employment for purposes of the 78-week test.

On a joint return, only one spouse is required to meet the time test.

If you expect to satisfy the time test, you can claim the deduction on your return even though you have not yet satisfied it.

Example

You move in August 2008 to a job in another state. By the end of 2008 you have completed only 20 weeks of full-time work in your new workplace. You can deduct your moving expenses on your 2008 return as long as you anticipate staying on the job for at least another 19 weeks.

If you don't claim the deduction in the year of the move, you must then file an amended return to claim the moving expense deduction. But if you claim the deduction on your return for the year of the move but later fail to satisfy the time test, you can either:

- Amend your return, eliminating the deduction you had claimed.
- Report as income in the year you should have met the time test but didn't the deduction you claimed on the earlier return.

If you expected to meet the time test, you don't have to report the deduction as income if the failure was due to:

- Disability that results in job termination.
- Job termination because you are laid off or fired for a reason other than willful misconduct.
- A permanent change of station if you are in the armed forces.
- Being a retiree or survivor of a person living outside the United States. If your old workplace and old home were both outside the United States, a move home is deductible (you don't have to meet any time test). Similarly, if you are the spouse or dependent of someone whose principal workplace was outside the United States at the time of his or her death, your moving costs are deductible without regard to the time test if the move begins within six months of the death and you lived with the person at the time of his or her death.
- Death. In other words, if someone claimed a moving expense deduction but died before meeting the time test, there is no income recapture of the benefit.

Planning Tip

Even though you can deduct your moving costs, it still makes sense to keep them as low as possible. When planning a move, to get a rough idea of moving costs, use The Moving Calculator from Realtor.com (www.homefair.com/home fair/calc/moveclacin.html). Be sure to get several binding quotes from reputable moving companies before contracting with one of them. Finally, put everything you agree to in writing and include adequate insurance for loss, breakage, and other damage. Learn about moving, including how to insure the move, in *The Moving Guide* from MovingGuru (www.movingguru.com).

Pitfalls

You cannot claim a moving expense deduction if you are relocating because of retirement (other than in the case of the armed forces). For example, if you sell your business in New York and retire to Florida, the cost of the move is a nondeductible personal expense.

You cannot deduct the costs of a move to start your first job after you've completed your education, even if you've held summer or part-time jobs during school. For example, if you graduate from college in California in June 2006 and accept a position in Washington, D.C., you cannot deduct your moving expenses; you don't have an old workplace from which to measure your move.

Not every move-related expense is deductible.

EXAMPLES OF NONDEDUCTIBLE MOVING EXPENSES
- Any part of the purchase price of a new home
- Car registration tags
- Driver's license
- Expenses of buying or selling a home
- Expenses of getting or breaking a lease
- Home improvements to sell your home
- Losses from disposing of club memberships
- Meal expenses

- Mortgage penalties (but they may be deductible as an itemized mortgage interest expense as explained earlier in this chapter)
- Premove house-hunting expenses
- Real estate taxes (but they may be deductible as an itemized expense)
- Refitting of carpets and draperies
- Security deposits forfeited
- Storage charges except those incurred in transit and for foreign moves
- Temporary living expenses

Where to Claim the Deduction

If your employer pays your moving costs and you are eligible to exclude this benefit from your income, you do not report them on your return.

If you deduct your expenses, figure the deduction on Form 3903, Moving Expenses, which you attach to your return. Enter the deductible amount in the "Adjusted Gross Income" section of Form 1040.

You cannot claim a moving expense deduction if you file Form 1040A or Form 1040EZ.

Energy Improvements

The Energy Tax Incentives Act of 2005 created tax credits for homeowners who make certain energy-saving improvements. In view of currently high energy costs, which are expected to remain high (at least for some time), consider taking advantage of tax breaks to save money on taxes and energy costs.

Benefit ⊕

There are several tax credits that a homeowner may claim for making certain energy improvements to the home. These include a 10 percent credit for adding qualified energy efficiency improvements and a 30 percent credit for solar energy and fuel cell power plants.

Conditions

The law requires that these improvements meet certain energy-saving standards and cannot exceed certain dollar limits. Different requirements apply to energy improvements and to solar energy and fuel cell power plants.

ENERGY IMPROVEMENTS

To qualify for the 10 percent credit, energy improvements must meet or exceed the criteria established by the 2000 International Energy Conservation Code (including supplements) and must be installed in your main home in the United States. This residential energy break expired at the end of 2007; But applies again in 2009.

ELIGIBLE ITEMS

These include:

- Insulation systems that reduce heat loss/gain
- Exterior windows (including skylights)
- Exterior doors
- Metal roofs treated with special paint (meeting applicable Energy Star requirements)
- Advanced main air circulating fan (up to $50)

- Qualified natural gas, propane, or oil furnace or hot water heater (up to $150)
- Each item of qualified energy-efficient property (up to $300)

LIMITATIONS

In addition to the dollar limits listed, the maximum credit for all taxable years is $500. No more than $200 of the credit can be attributable to expenses for windows.

SOLAR POWER AND FUEL CELLS

To qualify for the 30 percent credit, which runs through 2008 and may be extended even longer, solar panels, solar water heating equipment, or a fuel cell power plant must be added to your main home in the United States.

In general, a qualified fuel cell power plant converts a fuel into electricity using electrochemical means, has an electricity-only generation efficiency of more than 30 percent, and generates at least 0.5 kilowatts of electricity.

You can claim one credit equal to 30 percent of the qualified investment in a solar panel up to a maximum credit of $2,000, and another equivalent credit for investing in a solar water heating system.

Additionally, you are allowed a 30 percent tax credit for the purchase of qualified fuel cell power plants. The credit may not exceed $500 for each 0.5 kilowatt of capacity.

Planning Tips

The credit applies only to improvements made before the end of 2008.

Starting in 2009, there is a residential energy credit for small wind investment and geothermal heat pumps.

Pitfalls

Not every energy-saving measure qualifies for a credit. For purposes of the energy improvements credit, siding does not qualify. For purposes of the solar or fuel cell power plant credit, no part of either system can be used to heat a pool or hot tub.

You must reduce the basis of your home by the amount of any energy credit claimed. For example, if you claimed a $200 tax credit in 2007 for installing new storm doors, you must subtract $200 from the basis of your home.

Where to Claim the Credits

You figure the credit on Form 5965, Residential Energy Credits. The credit is then entered in the "Tax and Credits" section of Form 1040, or in the "Tax, Credits, and Payments" section of Form 1040A. You may not claim the credit if you file Form 1040EZ.

CHAPTER 5

Your Business

The United States is an entrepreneurial country—it is the American dream to own your own business, and millions already do. It has been estimated that there are now nearly 26 million small businesses (nearly 20 million of which are sole proprietorships). Most expenses related to running a business are deductible, but timing issues and limitations may come into play. The tax rules for your business apply whether you operate a full-time or a sideline business. This chapter deals primarily with business deductions for a sole proprietor who files Schedule C (or, for farming, Schedule F). Of course, many rules discussed in this chapter apply to partnerships, limited liability companies, and corporations.

This chapter explains:

- Start-up costs
- Equipment purchases
- Payment for services
- Supplies
- Gifts
- Hobby losses
- Self-employment tax deduction
- Home office deduction
- Farming-related breaks
- Domestic production activities deduction
- Other business deductions
- Other business credits
- Net operating losses

Retirement plans for self-employed individuals are discussed in Chapter 5.

For more information, see IRS Publication 15, *Circular E, Employer's Tax Guide;* IRS Publication 225, *Farmer's Tax Guide;* IRS Publication 334, *Tax Guide for Small Business;* IRS Publication 535, *Business Expenses;* IRS Publication 536, *Net Operating Losses;* IRS Publication 587, *Business Use of Your Home;* and IRS Publication 946, *How to Depreciate Property*. Also see *J.K. Lasser's Small Business Taxes 2009*, by Barbara Weltman.

Start-up Costs

The term "start-up" has a very specific meaning for tax purposes. When you think of the start-up phase of a business, you typically think about the first few years of operation when the business gets going. But for tax purposes, start-up means that period of time just *before* you actually focus on the business you then begin. It is the period in which you are looking for a business to go into.

Benefit ①

When you decide to start a business, you may incur certain costs. Usually, these costs are viewed as capital expenditures that are not currently deductible. But you can deduct up to $5,000 of start-up costs in the year the business begins. If start-up costs exceed $5,000, the balance can be amortized (deducted ratably) over 180 months.

If start-up costs exceed $50,000, the $5,000 deduction limit is reduced dollar for dollar by the excess over $50,000. If start-up costs exceed $55,000, no immediate deduction is allowed; such costs can be amortized over 180 months.

Conditions

Start-up expenses include costs related to deciding *whether* to go into business and which business to buy or start. This is referred to as the "whether and which" test.

EXAMPLES OF START-UP COSTS

- A survey of potential markets
- Advertisements for the opening of the business
- An analysis of available facilities, labor, and supplies
- Salaries and fees for consultants and executives
- Travel and other expenses incurred to get prospective distributors, suppliers, and customers

Expenses incurred after the start-up phase that relate to starting the business cannot be amortized; they must be capitalized (added to the cost of the business).

Example

You find a business you want to purchase and ask your accountant to review the company's books. Then you ask your attorney to draw up a contract of sale. Since you have already identified a particular business, you are beyond the start-up phase for tax purposes and accountant's and attorney's fees cannot be currently deducted or amortized as part of start-up expenses; they are simply part of the basis (cost) of your business, along with the purchase price of the company.

Planning Tips

Remember to keep track of your annual deductible amount so you don't overlook the write-off opportunity in the coming years.

If you sell your business before the end of the amortization period (assuming your start-up costs were not initially fully deducted), you can deduct any unamortized amount in the final year of business.

The same $5,000 deduction limit and 180-month amortization period applies to certain other expenses you may incur in forming a business: incorporation costs and partnership organizational costs. Like start-up costs, make sure that the items fit within the write-off category and then apply the $5,000 deduction limit and 180-month amortization rule.

Pitfall

Start-up costs are limited to expenses incurred *before* you begin operations. Once you have passed the start-up phase, which means you've identified the business or type of business you'll start, you can no longer include expenses in your pot of start-up expenses.

Where to Claim the Benefit

Report the amortizable amount of your start-up costs on Schedule C (or Schedule F) as "Other expenses." If you have more than one expense, you must list each of them in the space provided for this on Schedule C (or Schedule F).

You cannot claim a deduction for start-up expenses if you file Form 1040A or 1040EZ.

Equipment Purchases

It usually takes more than just your brains and hard work to make a business run. You need equipment, from technology-based items (e.g., computers and cell phones), to furniture (e.g., desks, file cabinets, and chairs), to industry-specific items (e.g., carpentry tools and heavy machinery). For tax purposes, all of these items are viewed as "equipment" for which special tax treatment may be claimed. Today, the tax law encourages investments in equipment as a means of spurring the economy by allowing an immediate deduction for purchase costs if certain conditions are met.

Benefit 🛈

You can deduct as an ordinary business expense amounts you pay for equipment used in your business. However, tax law dictates when and how much of your cost you can deduct. Three sets of rules come into play:

1. *First-year expensing.* Up to $250,000 can be deducted in the year the equipment is placed in service. Higher dollar limits apply for equipment placed in service in certain distressed areas; a lower dollar limit applies for vehicles weighing more than 6,000 pounds.

2. *Bonus depreciation.* Fifty percent of the cost of equipment may be deducted if purchased and placed in service in 2008. There is no dollar limit on bonus depreciation, but it applies only to new property. Qualifying property includes equipment and certain leasehold improvements.

3. *Depreciation.* A percentage of the equipment's basis is deducted over a set term (a recovery period fixed for various types of assets). There is no dollar limit on depreciation.

Conditions

Equipment purchases are not limited to machinery; the term "equipment" includes just about any type of property other than real estate.

EXAMPLES OF EQUIPMENT

- Answering machine
- Bookshelves
- Cars
- Cell phones
- Computers
- Copiers
- Desk accessories
- Desk chairs
- Desks
- Farming equipment (see later in this chapter)
- Fax machines
- File cabinets
- Floor models and displays
- Machinery
- Musical instruments for musicians
- Printers
- Signs
- Software purchased off-the-shelf
- Telephones
- Tools of your trade
- Trucks
- Vacuum cleaner

Different conditions apply to the different ways in which you can write off equipment purchases. You can combine these write-offs to maximize your deduction.

Example

In June 2008, you purchase a reconditioned machine costing $300,000 (assume the machine is classified under the tax law as five-year property and this is your only purchase for the year). You can deduct a total of $260,000 ($250,000 + $10,000):

First-year expensing of $250,000.

Regular depreciation of $10,000 ([$300,000 − $250,000] × 20%).

Bonus depreciation does not apply because the property is not new.

The rules on depreciation are quite complex, and a complete discussion is well beyond the scope of this chapter. Here you will gain an overview of the rules that apply. To learn more, see IRS Publication 946, *How to Depreciate Property*.

Conditions for First-Year Expensing

There are three basic conditions for claiming first-year expensing:

1. You must elect it.
2. Your total equipment purchases for the year cannot exceed a set dollar amount.
3. Your taxable income must at least equal your expense deduction.

ELECTION

You must elect to claim first-year expensing (also referred to as a Section 179 deduction because of the section in the Internal Revenue Code governing the deduction).

EQUIPMENT PURCHASES

To qualify for the election, your total equipment purchases for the year cannot exceed a set dollar amount. For 2008, you can claim the $250,000 expensing deduction only if your total purchases are no more than $800,000. The dollar limit phases out on a dollar-for-dollar basis so that no expensing deduction can be claimed if total purchases exceed $1,050,000.

TAXABLE INCOME

Your first-year expensing deduction cannot be more than the taxable income from the active conduct of a business. Taxable income for this purpose means your net income (or loss) from all businesses you actively conduct. If you are married and file a joint return, your spouse's net income (or loss) is added to yours. Taxable income also includes Section 1231 gains and losses (from the sale of certain business property) and salary or wages from being an employee. Taxable income must be reduced by the deduction for one-half of self-employment tax and net operating loss carrybacks and carryforwards.

Example

You own a sole proprietorship that shows a $5,000 profit for the year, and your deduction for one-half of self-employment tax is $383. Your spouse works as an employee with a salary of $50,000. Your taxable income for purposes of figuring your first-year expensing deduction is $54,617 ($5,000 − $383 + $50,000).

Conditions for Depreciation

Depreciation is a method for recovering your investment in property over a period of time fixed by law, called a recovery period. You apply a set percentage (based on the property's recovery period) to the property's basis (generally its cost) to arrive at your annual deduction. These percentages may be found in IRS Publication 946.

Example

In 2008, you place in service a copier machine (five-year property) for which you do not claim any first-year expensing or bonus depreciation. Assume the cost of the machine is $8,000. Your depreciation percentage for the year that five-year property is placed in service is 20 percent, so your depreciation deduction is $1,600 ($8,000 × 20%).

Different types of property are classified by their recovery periods:

- Three-year property, such as taxis, tractors, racehorses over two years old when placed in service, and breeding hogs

- Five-year property, such as cars, trucks, copiers, assets used in construction, and breeding and dairy cattle
- Seven-year property, such as office fixtures and furniture, fax machines, assets used in printing, assets used in recreation (e.g., billiard tables), and breeding horses and workhorses

There are also 10-year, 15-year, and 20-year types of property as well as realty (27.5 years for residential realty and 39 years for nonresidential realty such as office buildings, strip malls, and factories).

CONVENTIONS

Special depreciation rules, called conventions, come into play to determine your write-offs for the year.

- For property other than realty, a midyear convention makes a hypothetical assumption that the property has been placed in service in the middle of the year. As a result of the midyear convention, five-year property is depreciated over six years.
- For property other than realty, a midquarter convention applies. If you place in service more than 40 percent of all your equipment purchases for the year in the final quarter of the year, a special rule dictates the amount of depreciation you can claim for each item placed in service during the year. This special rule is called a midquarter convention and generally operates to limit write-offs (although in some cases it may enable you to take greater deductions than under regular depreciation rules).

- For realty, a midmonth convention assumes that the property has been placed in service in the middle of the month it is actually placed in service. The midmonth convention is built into the depreciation rate tables applied to realty.

Planning Tips

The amount of your write-offs does not depend on whether you pay cash for the equipment or finance your purchase. If, for example, you finance your purchase, you may wind up deducting more in the first year than you pay out of pocket.

Example

In December 2008, you buy a machine for $25,000, financing it over five years at 8 percent interest. In 2008, you can claim a first-year expensing deduction of $25,000, even though you have not yet paid a penny.

Decide whether to make the first-year expensing election and/or forego bonus depreciation. Generally, if your current income is modest but you expect it to increase in coming years, it may be preferable to forgo the deduction now in favor of using it against future income that would otherwise be taxed at higher rates.

Pitfalls

Special rules apply to so-called "listed property," which includes cars, computers and peripherals not used at a regular business establishment, and cell phones. You cannot use first-year expensing or accelerated depreciation *unless* business use of a listed property item is more than 50 percent of total use.

Example

You buy a cell phone that is used 75 percent for business and 25 percent for personal purposes. Since business use exceeds 50 percent, you can use first-year expensing or accelerated depreciation for the portion of the phone (75 percent of its purchase price) used for business.

If you sell or cease using property for which first-year expensing has been claimed, you *may* be subject to recapture. This means you're required to report a portion of the previous write-off as income in the year of the disposition of the property. Discuss this rather complicated matter with a tax adviser.

Where to Claim the Deduction

You figure your deduction for equipment purchases on Form 4562, Depreciation and Amortization. You enter the amount of your deduction on the line provided for this write-off on Schedule C (or Schedule F).

If you are claiming depreciation this year on an item placed in service in a prior year and you do not have any new items to report, you do not have to file Form 4562. Simply attach your own schedule to the return showing the amount of depreciation you are claiming this year.

You cannot claim a deduction for equipment purchases if you file Form 1040A or 1040EZ.

Payment for Services

You may not be able to do it alone and may therefore need to hire employees to work for your business. The costs of wages, salaries, bonuses, and other payments are deductible if certain conditions are met.

Benefit

Amounts you pay to individuals who provide services to you are deductible as ordinary expenses against your business income. Such payments fall into two general categories:

1. Wages and compensation to employees.
2. Fees and payments to independent contractors.

There are no dollar limits on the amount you can deduct for payments for services.

In addition to a deduction for wages and compensation to employees, you may be eligible to claim a tax credit for a portion of these payments.

Conditions

There are several conditions for determining how much to deduct for payments to workers:

- It must be determined whether the worker is an employee or independent contractor.
- Amounts paid must be reasonable.

- Payment must relate to work actually performed.
- Payments must be made in a timely fashion.
- Employer credit for wage differential payments to activated reservists after June 17, 2008.

WORKER CLASSIFICATION

First you must determine whether workers are your employees or independent contractors. The key reason for making the distinction is the obligation to pay employment taxes—Social Security and Medicare (FICA) taxes, federal unemployment insurance (FUTA), and state unemployment and other payroll taxes. If you are the employer, you are responsible for the employer's share of taxes as well as withholding income taxes and the employee's share of FICA. If your worker is an independent contractor, then he or she is responsible for employment taxes.

Generally, worker classification as an employee or independent contractor is based on control. If you control when, where, and how work is to be performed, the person is your employee regardless of what label you may attach. If the person is in his or her own business and provides services to you, the person usually is treated as an independent contractor.

REASONABLE PAYMENTS

Compensation paid to your employees must be "reasonable." There's no set dollar amount. Reasonable depends on many factors, including job responsibilities, education level, and location of the business. Payments to yourself as a sole proprietor are not treated as deductible compensation because you are not an employee.

Payments paid to independent contractors must also be reasonable.

PERFORMANCE OF WORK

You can deduct only payments for work actually performed. Generally, this poses no problem for your rank-and-file employees. But if you put family members on the payroll, the IRS may look closely at the relation between their wages and work performed. Keep track of the hours they worked and the tasks they performed as proof they earned the compensation you paid.

TIMELINESS OF PAYMENT

You can deduct only payments you actually make (if you are on the cash method of accounting for your business). If you are on the accrual method, payments to rank-and-file employees must be made no later than two-and-a-half months after the close of the year (e.g., by March 15, 2009, for compensation earned in 2008). (Different rules apply to payments to shareholders in C and S corporations.)

Planning Tip

Compensation paid to certain employees may entitle you to claim a tax credit (more details may be found later in this chapter). These include:

- Work opportunity credit for workers within several targeted groups.
- Empowerment zone credit for workers within designated areas.

- Indian employment credit for workers on Indian reservations.

- Social Security tax credit on certain tips for workers in restaurant and tavern businesses.

Pitfall

If your workers are employees, you are responsible for employment taxes. This requires you to withhold federal and, if applicable, state income taxes from their wages, as well as the employee share of FICA tax. You must also pay the employer share of FICA as well as FUTA and state employment taxes. If you fail to pay over these taxes in a timely fashion, you may be personally liable for them.

Where to Claim the Deduction

You report the deduction for compensation to employees on the line designated as "Wages" on Schedule C of Form 1040. Wages are reduced by employment tax credits you claim (listed earlier in "Planning Tip"). You report payments to independent contractors on the line marked "Commissions and fees" of this schedule.

For farming-related activities, the deduction for wages to employees is reported on the line marked "Labor hired" on Schedule F of Form 1040. Wages are reduced by employment tax credits you claim. You report payments to independent contractors on the line marked "Customer hire" of this schedule.

Employment tax credits to which you may be entitled are figured on the following forms:

- Work opportunity credit: Form 5884.

- Empowerment zone credit: Form 8844.

- Indian employment credit: Form 8845.
- Social Security tax credit on certain tips: Form 8846.
- Credit for employer wage differential payments: Form 8932.

Supplies

To paraphrase Benjamin Franklin, for want of a paper clip your business may be lost. Despite predictions of a paperless society, most businesses use reams of paper and other supplies every year. The tax law allows a full write-off for the cost of ordinary supplies as long as certain conditions are met.

Benefit 🛈

Office supplies (including paper, pens, tape, and toner replacements) and cleaning supplies (such as detergent, paper towels, and sponges) are deductible against your business income. There is no dollar limit on this deduction.

Supplies that are part of your inventory are *not* currently deductible; they are part of the cost of goods sold.

Conditions

For supplies to be currently deductible, they must be ordinary and necessary business expenses. They cannot be items with a useful life of more than one year. If they have a longer useful life, they are treated as equipment (discussed later in this chapter).

EXAMPLES OF DEDUCTIBLE SUPPLIES

- Binders and presentation material
- Boards and easels

- Business cards
- Cleaning supplies
- Diskettes, CDs, and zip disks
- Filing and storage material
- Ink cartridges and toners
- Labels, envelopes, and shipping material
- Paper clips, tape, and staples
- Paper, pads, and notes
- Pens, pencils, and markers
- Replacement parts (which are not part of inventory)
- Rubber stamps
- Small wares of restaurants and taverns (e.g., glassware, paper or plastic cups, dishes, pots and pans, and bar supplies)
- Stationery
- Trash bags

Planning Tips

From a nontax standpoint, it may not make economic sense to load up on supplies even though you can deduct them. You are incurring costs now that could be paid later.

While the cost of supplies generally is deductible, it is a good business practice to economize on purchases. Look for discounts and special business incentives from such office supplies companies as:

- Office Depot (www.officedepot.com)
- Office Max (www.officemax.com)
- Staples (www.staples.com)

Pitfalls

Supplies that are part of your inventory are *not* separately deducted. Instead, they are included as part of your cost of goods sold.

Watch the timing of ordering supplies. A current deduction is allowed for supplies used within the year. A deduction for supplies *not* used within the current year but kept on hand may still be claimed as long as doing so does not distort income, no records are maintained to indicate when supplies are actually used, and no inventory is taken of the amount of supplies on hand at the beginning and end of the year.

Where to Claim the Benefit

Report supplies used in your business on the line provided for this item on Schedule C (or Schedule F) of Form 1040. You do not have to complete any additional form or schedule for this purpose.

You cannot deduct business supplies if you file Form 1040A or Form 1040EZ.

Gifts

Gifts generally are given because of personal feelings without any expectations or strings attached. But business gifts usually are motivated by gratitude for some business activity or hope for future business activity. In recognition of this fact, the tax law allows a deduction for business gifts, but only in very limited amounts.

Benefit ①

You may wish to bestow some gratuitous benefit on employees, customers, dealers, distributors, or other business relations. You can qualify for a deduction for business gifts, but the amount you can deduct is limited. Generally, you cannot deduct more than $25 per gift for any person each year (the same dollar limit in place since 1954). The dollar limit applies even if you attempt to make an indirect gift (for example, you give the gift to a company that is intended for the eventual personal use of a particular person).

Conditions

To claim a deduction for business gifts, you must meet both of the following conditions:

1. Dollar limit
2. Substantiation

DOLLAR LIMIT

The deductible amount of the gift cannot exceed $25 per person per year. The dollar limit does not include incidental costs, such as wrapping, insuring, or shipping the gift.

Example

You give a new vendor a gift that cost you $60. You paid $10 more to insure and ship it. You can deduct $35 ($25 of the $60, plus incidental expenses of $10).

In determining your $25 annual limit, you do not have to count any gifts of nominal value ($4 or less) with your company name imprinted on them that you distribute to a number of clients or customers (e.g., calendars at Christmastime).

SUBSTANTIATION REQUIREMENTS

You must show the cost of the gift, a description of the gift, the date it was given, and to whom. You must also state the reason for the gift (such as the business to be gained from making it). This information should be recorded on an expense log or business diary.

In addition, you must have evidentiary proof of the expense, such as a canceled check or receipt for the item.

Planning Tips

Gifts to your employees are *not* subject to this $25 limit because payments to them usually are treated as compensation (discussed earlier in this chapter). As long as regular compensation plus any purported gifts are reasonable, the total is deductible as compensation.

Certain items can be treated as gifts, such as an entertainment expense, which is *not* subject to the $25 limit. You have the option of using this treatment if you give tickets to the theater or a sports event and do *not* attend the event yourself. In making the choice, keep in mind that the entertainment deduction is subject to a 50 percent limit (without regard to a dollar amount).

Example

You buy your best customer tickets to a local golf tournament for $80. Assuming you do not attend, you are better off treating the ticket as an entertainment expense so you can deduct $40 (50% of $80), rather than as a business gift, which would be deductible at only $25.

If you treat the ticket as a business gift, you have three years in which to change your mind and file an amended return to report the ticket as an entertainment expense.

If you give food or a beverage intended to be consumed by your customer or other businessperson, you *must* treat the item as a gift (you do not have the choice to treat it as an entertainment expense).

Pitfall

You must substantiate your business gifts in order to support your deduction. If you fail to meet full substantiation requirements, your deduction is lost. For example, merely retaining a receipt for the gift is not sufficient; you need to note all the information listed earlier as full substantiation for the gift.

Where to Claim the Deduction

You report the gifts as "Other expenses" on Schedule C (or Schedule F) of Form 1040. If you have more than one such expense (for example, in addition to business gifts, you are deducting environmental cleanup costs), you must list each type of expense in the space provided (or on your own attachment if more space is required).

You cannot deduct any business gifts if you file Form 1040A or 1040EZ.

Hobby Losses

When does a hobby become a business? The tax law says this happens when you are profitable. In effect, if you lose money you bear the cost entirely, but if you make money the government shares in your good fortune. You can deduct losses from activities that might be viewed as hobbies only under certain conditions.

Benefit ⬒

If you do not have a profit motive for running an activity—especially one involving some element of personal recreation or pleasure, such as coin collecting or dog breeding—then your expenses are deductible only to the extent of your income from the activity. The hobby loss rule acts as a limitation on your deductions—dictating how much you can deduct and where to claim the deduction for your business expenses.

Hobby losses are treated as miscellaneous itemized deductions, which are deductible only to the extent they exceed 2 percent of adjusted gross income.

Conditions

You want to avoid application of the hobby loss rule so that your business expenses in excess of business income are deductible. If your business is unprofitable year after year, the IRS may question whether you are in it for a profit or are merely trying to deduct the costs of a hobby.

To avoid the hobby loss rule, you must be able to demonstrate that you are in the activity to make a profit. Of course, this is a subjective determination based on your reasonable expectations and beliefs. But certain objective criteria are used to show you really mean business. No single factor is determinative; the more you can muster, the better off you will be:

- You run the activity in a businesslike manner (e.g., keep good records separate from your personal activities and have a business bank account, telephone, stationery, and other indications of a business).
- You put in substantial time and effort.
- You depend on income from the activity for your livelihood (if you have other sources of income, this tends to show the activity is merely a hobby).
- You consult with advisers to make the business profitable.
- You have profits in some years (the bounty in your good years can support a profit motive).
- You expect to see a profit from the appreciation of assets used in the activity.

Planning Tips

You can opt to rely on a presumption that you are in the activity for a profit—opting for this presumption delays any IRS inquiry about your activity. You are presumed to be in an activity for profit if you make a profit for at least three of the first five years you are in business (two out of seven years if the activity is breeding, training, showing, or racing horses).

To use the presumption, you must file Form 5213, Election to Postpone Determination as to Whether the Presumption Applies That an Activity Is Engaged In for Profit. The form can be filed with the first return for your activity; it must be filed within three years of the due date of the return for the first year of the activity.

Of course, the downside to making this election to postpone inquiry into your activity is that you are extending the statute of limitations under which the IRS may question your deductions. Generally the IRS has only three years, but filing Form 5213 means they have five years—and you can expect to have your returns examined at the end of the five-year period.

If you make the election but fail the presumption, you are not precluded from arguing you really had a profit motive, even though you had losses in many years. One of the key ways to show a profit motive is to have a written business plan spelling out how you expect to make the activity profitable and when you anticipate that this will occur.

Pitfall

The hobby loss rule applies to individuals, including partners and members of limited liability companies; it does not apply to C corporations. In the case of pass-through entities, the determination of a profit motive is made at the entity level (for example, you might be in a partnership to make a profit but it is up to the partnership to prove it has a profit motive).

Where to Claim the Benefit

If you are subject to the hobby loss rule, you report your income from the activity as other income in the "Income" section of Form 1040 and expenses from the activity as miscellaneous itemized deductions on Schedule A of Form 1040.

You cannot claim any hobby loss deduction if you file Form 1040A or 1040EZ.

Self-Employment Tax Deduction

Self-employed individuals pay both the employer and employee share of Social Security and Medicare taxes. But self-employed persons are treated as their own employers to the extent they are permitted to deduct the employer share of these taxes.

Benefit ①

If you pay self-employment tax on your net earnings from self-employment, you can deduct one-half of the liability as an adjustment to gross income, even if you do not itemize your other deductions.

Conditions

Self-employment tax is the employer and employee share of Social Security and Medicare taxes figured on your net earnings from self-employment. As long as you show a profit in your self-employment activities, you owe self-employment tax and can deduct the portion representing the employer share (one-half of the total tax).

Planning Tip

To figure your deduction, simply look at Schedule SE, Self-Employment Tax, the form used to figure your self-employment tax. The last line of the short or long form of Schedule SE allows you to figure your deduction by multiplying your self-employment tax by 50 percent.

Pitfall

The deduction for one-half of your self-employment tax is *not* a business expense, but a personal one. It does not reduce your profits on which you pay income and self-employment taxes.

Where to Claim the Benefit

You report the deduction on the line provided in the "Adjusted Gross Income" section of Form 1040. No separate form or schedule is required for this purpose.

Home Office Deduction

The number of home-based businesses is put between 18 million and 38 million; exact figures are not available because the U.S. Census Bureau failed to question whether full-time employees also had home-based businesses. Whatever the number, the cost of operating an office from home may be deductible as long as certain conditions are met. The term "home office" isn't limited to clerical space; it can include a workshop, greenhouse, artist studio, or any other area of a home used for business.

Benefit ①

Whether you work exclusively at a home-based business or operate a sideline business from home, you may be able to deduct a portion of your housing costs, including depreciation if you own your home or rent if you lease it, plus utilities, insurance, maintenance, and other related costs. (Congress may add a standard deduction for home offices in lieu of deducting actual expenses, so check the Supplement for details.) The deduction serves to offset your business income.

There are two types of expenses related to a home office:

1. Indirect expenses (the portion of the general expenses of running your home)
2. Direct expenses (costs incurred solely in your home office)

Example

You paint the outside of your home for $8,000. If your home office is 10 percent of your home, then $800 of this cost is an indirect expense. If you paid $800 to paint the home office itself, it is entirely deductible (no allocation is required) because it is a direct expense.

In the case of indirect expenses, you must allocate them between the residence and office portion of the home. Usually home office space for purposes of making an allocation is figured on a square footage basis (e.g., if your home is 2,400 square feet and you use 240 square feet as a home office, then 10 percent of your indirect expenses become part of your home office deduction).

Conditions

To claim a home office deduction, you must meet all three of these conditions:

1. Principal place of business or other acceptable use
2. Regular and exclusive use
3. Gross income requirement

PRINCIPAL PLACE OF BUSINESS OR OTHER ACCEPTABLE USE

Your home office must be one of the following:

- Your principal place of business, which is generally the place at which you conduct your business and generate income from the business activity. This includes using your office for substantial administrative or managerial activities for which you have no other fixed location.
- A place to meet or deal with clients, customers, or patients in the normal course of your business.
- A separate structure (such as a freestanding garage) that is used *in connection with* your business.

REGULAR AND EXCLUSIVE USE

The portion of your home used for business must be used for this purpose regularly and exclusively. This means that you can't use your den as an office by day and a family room by night.

You do not need to use an entire room or physically partition space within a room; you only need to devote whatever space you use for business entirely for this purpose.

GROSS INCOME REQUIREMENT

Your home office deduction cannot exceed gross income from the home office activity. Gross income for this purpose generally means your profits reported on Schedule C (or Schedule F) from the activity for which the home office is used.

If you have a bad year, your deduction may be limited (the ordering of what expenses you can claim is figured by following the line-by-line instructions to Form 8829, Expenses for Business Use of Your Home).

If after applying this ordering of deductions you still have unused expenses, you can carry forward this unused amount. There is no time limit on this carryfoward. You can use it when you have income *from the same activity that generated the deduction*, whether or not you are still in the same home at the time of earning that income.

Example

In 2007, your sole proprietorship in the landscaping business reported a loss so that your $2,300 home office deduction could not be claimed. In 2008, your landscaping business becomes profitable enough to allow you to deduct the $2,300 carryforward (plus any home office deduction for 2008). You could still deduct the $2,300 even if you moved to a new residence in 2008.

Planning Tips

Claiming a home office deduction entitles you to certain ancillary benefits:

- Travel to and from your home for business is deductible (there's no such thing as commuting when you have a home office)
- A computer used in the home office is *not* treated as listed property (you do not have to track the business use of the computer in order to claim first-year expensing or accelerated depreciation as discussed earlier in this chapter)

Claiming a home office deduction does *not* taint your opportunity to exclude gain on the sale of your home. The tax law allows you to claim a home sale exclusion of up to $250,000 ($500,000 on a joint return) for the *entire* home (see Chapter 4 for more details).

It is advisable to take a photo of your home office, so that if your return is questioned, you can help to demonstrate exclusive business use of the space.

Pitfall

When you sell your home, you must recapture any depreciation claimed after May 6, 1997, on your home office. Recapture means that the amount becomes taxable at the rate of 25 percent (assuming you are in a tax bracket higher than 25 percent).

Where to Claim the Benefit

You figure the home office deduction on Form 8829, Expenses for Business Use of Your Home. The deduction is then entered on Schedule C (or Schedule F) of Form 1040 on the line provided for it.

If this is the first year in which you are claiming a home office deduction for a home you own, you must also complete Form 4562, Depreciation and Amortization, to figure the depreciation allowance for the year. In future years, you do not have to complete this form if you do not place any new property in service; you simply attach your own statement to the return showing how you figured the depreciation allowance entered on Form 8829.

You cannot claim a home office deduction if you file Form 1040A or 1040EZ.

Farming-Related Breaks

According to the U.S. Department of Agriculture, there were more than 2.08 million farms in the United States in 2007, although the exit rate from farming is between 9 and 10 percent annually. Farming is considered a type of business and is therefore entitled to deductions available to any other business. But the tax law provides special breaks just for farms.

Benefit ① ⊗ ⊕

If you operate a farm or farming activity, many of your costs are deductible against your farming income. In addition to any business expense you could claim in a nonfarming business, you may be entitled to special write-offs. Generally, there are no dollar limits on your farming-related deductions.

Some benefits payable to farmers may be tax free. And some expenses paid by farmers may qualify for a tax credit.

Conditions

Like other business expenses, farming-related deductions must be ordinary and necessary expenses.

EXAMPLES OF FARMING-RELATED DEDUCTIONS

- Chemicals
- Conservation expenses for soil and water
- Custom hire (machine work)
- Enhanced deduction for donations of conservation easements (100 percent of the contribution base, which is essentially adjusted gross income)
- Feed purchased (there are limits on how much you can deduct for feed to be consumed beyond this year)

- Fertilizers and lime
- Freight and trucking
- Gasoline, oil, and other fuel
- Ginning
- Hired labor (reduced by any employment-related tax credits discussed earlier in this chapter)
- Insect sprays and dusts
- Seeds and plants purchased
- Storage and warehousing
- Tying materials and containers
- Veterinary and breeding fees and medicine

Planning Tips

Some payments to farmers may be tax free. These include:

- Cost-sharing payments under The Conservation Reserve Program (CRP)
- Soil and water conservation assistance payments under a special federal program, which may run as high as $50,000
- Agricultural management assistance program payments

In addition to deductions for farming expenses, you may be eligible for certain tax credits related to farming. These include:

- Credit for federal excise tax paid on kerosene used in your home for heating, lighting, and cooking
- Credit for federal excise tax paid on gasoline, special motor fuels, and compressed natural gas used on a farm for farming purposes

- Credit for federal excise tax on fuels used in running stationary machines, for cleaning purposes, or in other off-highway vehicles

You can claim the credits on your return or claim a refund of the excise taxes you already paid. The credits and your options on claiming them are explained in more detail in IRS Publication 225, *Farmer's Tax Guide*.

Pitfall

Not all farming-related expenses are deductible. You may not deduct your personal living expenses, such as taxes, insurance, and repairs to your home.

Where to Claim Farming-Related Deductions

Report the deduction on the line provided for it on Schedule F of Form 1040. If there is no specific line for the type of deduction you are claiming, list it in the space provided for other expenses (attach your own explanation or description of the expense if not self-explanatory).

You cannot deduct farming-related expenses if you file Form 1040A or Form 1040EZ.

Domestic Production Activities Deduction

If your business makes something in the United States, whether it's by manufacturing, agriculture, mining extraction, construction, filming, software development, or certain other approved activities, you can claim a deduction that effectively reduces the tax rate you pay on your business profits. The best part of the deduction: You don't have to spend any separate money to get it (you are entitled to it because of your activities).

Benefit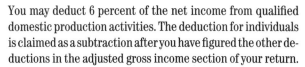

You may deduct 6 percent of the net income from qualified domestic production activities. The deduction for individuals is claimed as a subtraction after you have figured the other deductions in the adjusted gross income section of your return.

Conditions

There are several conditions to claiming this deduction:

- Derive income from a qualified activity
- Meet a W-2 limit
- Meet an adjusted gross income limit

QUALIFIED DOMESTIC ACTIVITY

You must derive the net income from a qualified activity, which includes:

- Selling, leasing, or licensing items manufactured, produced, grown, or extracted in the United States in whole or significant part (see safe harbor below).
- Selling, leasing, or licensing films produced in the United States.
- Construction in the United States Construction includes both erection and substantial renovation of residential and commercial buildings (but not cosmetic activities, such as painting).
- Engineering and architectural services relating to a construction project performed in the United States.

- Software developed in the United States, regardless of whether it is purchased off-the-shelf or downloaded from the Internet. The term *software* includes video games. But, with some *de minimis* exceptions, the term does not include fees for online use of software, fees for customer support, and fees for playing computer games online.

Under significant part safe harbor, you are treated as conducting activities in the United States if labor and overhead costs incurred in the United States for the manufacture, production, growth, and extraction of the property are at least 20 percent of the total cost of goods sold of the property.

Net income is figured by reducing gross receipts from qualified domestic activities by expenses allocated to these receipts. Under a de minimis rule, if less than 5 percent of total gross receipts is derived from nonqualified domestic production activities, you do not have to make any allocation; all gross receipts are treated as attributable to qualified domestic production activities.

If there is a service element in the activity, allocate gross receipts between the qualified activity and the services. However, no allocation is required if the gross receipts relate to a qualified warranty and other gross receipts from these services are 5 percent or less of the gross receipts from the property.

W-2 LIMIT

The deduction cannot exceed 50 percent of your business's W-2 wages paid in the calendar year that are allocable to domestic production activities. W-2 wages includes both taxable compensation and elective deferrals (e.g., employee contributions to 401(k) plans).

ADJUSTED GROSS INCOME LIMIT

The deduction cannot exceed your adjusted gross income.

Planning Tips

In order to increase your W-2 limitation, consider hiring employees rather than using independent contractors. Weigh the added cost of employment taxes against the tax savings derived from the higher production activities deduction because of additional W-2 wages.

If you are an owner of a pass-through entity (partnership, limited liability company, or S corporation), your share of the business's qualified production activities income and W-2 wages are reported on your Schedule K-1.

Pitfalls

You cannot claim the deduction if you lease or license property to a related party.

You cannot claim the deduction for the sale of food or beverages prepared at a retail establishment. However, if a business both manufactures food and sells it at a restaurant or take-out store, income and expenses can be allocated so that those related to manufacture and wholesale distribution qualify for the deduction. Thus, in the so-called "Starbucks" situation, roasting and packaging coffee beans could qualify, but selling the beans or brewed coffee at their stores would not.

Where to Claim the Deduction

The production activities deduction is figured on Form 8903, Domestic Production Activities Deduction, and is reported in the "Adjusted Gross Income" section of Form 1040. First report all of the other deductions in this section; then enter your production activities deduction (subject to the adjusted gross income limitation).

You cannot claim the deduction if you file Form 1040EZ or Form 1040A.

Other Business Deductions

Not every expense fits neatly into a business deduction category. The tax law provides a catchall deduction rule, referred to as the ordinary and necessary expense rule, under which an expense can be written off as long as certain conditions are met.

Benefit 🛈

A variety of miscellaneous expenses you incur in your business are currently deductible against business income.

Condition

The only condition for deductibility of miscellaneous expenses is that they are ordinary and necessary for your business. "Ordinary" means that they are usual. "Necessary" means they are helpful and appropriate.

EXAMPLES OF OTHER BUSINESS DEDUCTIONS

- Advertising costs—promotional costs as well as goodwill advertising to keep your name in the public eye.
- Asbestos removal.
- Banking fees.
- Depletion for certain oil, gas, and mineral as well as timber properties.

- Dues to professional and trade associations.
- Environmental cleanup costs—expenses to restore property to its precontamination condition.
- Insurance (for self-employed health insurance see Chapter 2).
- Intangibles (e.g., goodwill and covenant not to compete) that are acquired (must be amortized over 15 years).
- Interest on borrowing (for example, financing of equipment purchases).
- Leasing costs for equipment.
- Licenses and regulatory fees paid annually to state or local governments.
- Merchant authorization fees for credit card payments.
- Moving equipment and machinery.
- Rent for office and other business-related space.
- Repairs to keep property in working order (if repairs add to the value or usefulness of the property, the cost must be capitalized).
- Repayments of income reported in prior years. *Note:* If the amount of repayment is more than $3,000, you may be able to take a tax credit in lieu of a deduction to obtain a greater benefit from the write-off.
- Shipping and postage.
- Storage and warehousing.
- Subscriptions
- Telephone. If you operate your business from a home office, the basic service charge of the first line to your home is not deductible. But this ban does not apply to additional charges, such as business long-distance calls and

the cost of a second business line. The monthly cost of cell phone use is deductible (treatment of the purchase of a cell phone is discussed earlier in this chapter).

- Utilities. Gas, electric, water, and other charges are deductible. If you claim a home office deduction, the treatment of these charges is discussed earlier in this chapter.

Planning Tip

As with all business expenses, keep good records, including receipts, canceled checks, and bills of sale.

Pitfall

Not all expenses you incur in your business are deductible. The tax law specifically prevents you from writing off certain expenses, even though they may be ordinary and necessary to your business.

EXAMPLES OF NONDEDUCTIBLE EXPENSES

- Bribes and kickbacks—even if customary or common business practice, if they are in violation of the law. For example, an insurance broker who pays a "referral fee" to car dealers who refer customers to him cannot deduct the fee because the car dealers are not licensed to sell insurance.

- Club dues for clubs organized for pleasure, recreation, or any other social purpose. Exceptions to this rule are discussed in Chapter 10.

- Demolition expenses to raze a building. These costs are added to the basis of the land on which the building was demolished.

- Fines and penalties.

- Interest on a business-related tax deficiency.
- Lobbying expenses to influence legislation. *Exception:* Up to $2,000 of in-house costs for influencing legislation and communicating directly with a covered executive branch official can be deducted.

Where to Claim the Deduction

Deductible miscellaneous business expenses are reported on Schedule C (or Schedule F) either on the line provided for the type of expense (e.g., "Advertising" on Schedule C) or as "Other expenses." If you have more than one such expense, you must list each type of expense in the space provided (or on your own attachment if more space is required).

Net Operating Losses

Not every business can be profitable year in and year out. What happens if your business suffers a loss from its operations that effectively wipes out more than your tax liability for the year? You may then have what is called a net operating loss. You may be able to use this loss to reduce taxes in prior and/or future years.

Benefit ⬆

If your business expenses for the year outweigh your income, your loss may give rise to a net operating loss (NOL) that can be used to offset income in other tax years. Such loss can be carried back to offset income in prior years (producing an immediate tax refund); unused amounts can be carried forward to offset future income. There are limits on the carryback and carryforward years.

The net operating loss deduction is not an additional loss deduction. Rather it is the result of having deductions exceed your business income and applying this excess against income in other years.

Conditions

You must determine whether having a loss in your business for the year results in a net operating loss. You have an NOL if your adjusted gross income is a negative figure. But adjusted gross income for purposes of an NOL does not include certain deductions you are otherwise allowed to take. When figuring your NOL, increase your adjusted gross income by all of the following that apply to you:

- IRA deduction
- Alimony deduction
- Net capital losses (capital losses in excess of capital gains)
- Self-employed person's contribution to a qualified retirement plan

While this computation may sound complicated, you need only follow the line-by-line instructions to Form 1045, Application for Tentative Refund, to see how you adjust your income and determine your net operating loss.

CARRYBACK AND CARRYFORWARD PERIODS

The years to which you carry the loss backward and forward depend on the year in which the NOL arises.

- NOLs arising in tax years beginning before August 6, 1997, and after 2002: three years back; 15 years forward.

- NOLs arising in tax years beginning after August 5, 1997, and before January 1, 2001: generally two years back and 20 years forward. However, small businesses with average annual gross receipts of $5 million or less during a three-year period can use a three-year carryback for NOLs arising from federally declared disasters. For farmers and ranchers, as well as individuals and businesses in the disaster areas created by Hurricane Katrina, Rita, or Wilma, the 2008 Midwest floods, and Hurricane Ike, there is a five-year carryback. For NOLs arising from product liability, there is a 10-year carryback.

- NOLs arising in 2001 and 2002: five years back and 20 years forward.

Planning Tips

You can obtain a quick refund from an NOL carryback, money you can put into your business or use for any other purpose. To obtain a quick refund file Form 1045, Application for Tentative Refund, with the IRS. Usually you'll receive your refund within 90 days of filing the form.

Alternatively, you can obtain a refund by filing an amended return, Form 1040X.

You can elect to forgo the carryback and simply carry the NOL forward until it is used up. This election makes sense if you expect to be in a higher tax bracket in coming years than you were in prior years. Keep in mind, however, that tax rates are declining over the next several years.

Another reason to forgo the carryback is to avoid drawing attention to a prior year in which you may have taken a questionable tax position.

If you make the election to forgo the NOL carryback, it applies for alternative minimum tax purposes as well.

Be sure to keep track of NOLs arising in different years, especially since they may be subject to different carryback and carryforward periods.

Pitfalls

An NOL carryback does *not* allow you to refigure your self-employment tax and obtain a refund of that tax.

Net operating losses that are not used up within the carryforward period of 20 years are lost forever.

Where to Claim the Deduction

There is no special form required to be used in figuring a net operating loss. As a practical matter, you can figure your NOL on Schedule A of Form 1045.

A net operating loss is reported as a negative income item; it is not a direct offset to your business income. For example, if your net operating loss carryforward is $4,400, enter –4,400 on the "Other income" line in the "Income" section of Form 1040.